THE COMMUNE OF PARIS, 1871

MAJOR ISSUES IN HISTORY

Editor
C. WARREN HOLLISTER,
University of California, Santa Barbara

The Twelfth-Century Renaissance
C. Warren Hollister

The Impact of Absolutism in France:
National Experience under Richelieu, Mazarin, and Louis XIV
William F. Church

The Impact of the Norman Conquest
C. Warren Hollister

The Commune of Paris, 1871
Roger L. Williams

Relativity Theory:
Its Origins and Impact on Modern Thought
L. Pearce Williams

THE COMMUNE OF PARIS,
1871

EDITED BY

Roger L. Williams

John Wiley & Sons, Inc.
New York London Sydney Toronto

SERIES PREFACE

The reading program in a history survey course traditionally has consisted of a large two-volume textbook and, perhaps, a book of readings. This simple reading program requires few decisions and little imagination on the instructor's part, and tends to encourage in the student the virtue of careful memorization. Such programs are by no means things of the past, but they certainly do not represent the wave of the future.

The reading program in survey courses at many colleges and universities today is far more complex. At the risk of over-simplification, and allowing for many exceptions and overlaps, it can be divided into four categories: (1) textbook, (2) original source readings, (3) specialized historical essays and interpretive studies, and (4) historical problems.

After obtaining an overview of the course subject matter (textbook), sampling the original sources, and being exposed to selective examples of excellent modern historical writing (historical essays), the student can turn to the crucial task of weighing various possible interpretations of major historical issues. It is at this point that memory gives way to creative critical thought. The "problems approach," in other words, is the intellectual climax of a thoughtfully conceived reading program and is, indeed, the most characteristic of all approaches to historical pedagogy among the newer generation of college and university teachers.

The historical problems books currently available are many and varied. Why add to this information explosion? Because the Wiley Major Issues Series constitutes an endeavor to produce something new that will respond to pedagogical needs thus far unmet. First, it is a series of individual volumes—one per problem. Many good teachers would much prefer to select their own historical issues rather than be tied to an inflexible sequence of issues imposed by a publisher and bound together between two covers. Second, the Wiley Major Issues Series is based on the idea of approaching the significant problems of history through a deft interweaving of primary sources and secondary analysis, fused together by the skill of a scholar-editor. It is felt that the essence of a historical issue cannot be satisfactorily probed either by placing a body of undigested source materials into the hands of inexperienced students or by limiting these students to the controversial literature of modern scholars who debate the meaning of sources the student never sees. This series approaches historical problems by exposing students to both the finest historical thinking on the issue and some of the evidence on which this thinking is based. This synthetic approach should prove far more fruitful than either the raw-source approach or the exclusively second-hand approach, for it combines the advantages—and avoids the serious disadvantages—of both.

Finally, the editors of the individual volumes in the Major Issues Series have been chosen from among the ablest scholars in their fields. Rather than faceless referees, they are historians who know their issues from the inside and, in most instances, have themselves contributed significantly to the relevant scholarly literature. It has been the editorial policy of this series to permit the editor-scholars of the individual volumes the widest possible latitude both in formulating their topics and in organizing their materials. Their scholarly competence has been unquestioningly respected; they have been encouraged to approach the problems as they see fit. The titles and themes of the series volumes have been suggested in nearly every case by the scholar-editors themselves. The criteria have been (1) that the issue be of relevance to undergraduate lecture courses in history, and (2) that it be an issue which the scholar-editor knows thoroughly and in which he has done creative work. And, in general, the second criterion has been given precedence over the first. In short, the question "What are the significant historical issues today?" has been answered not by general editors or sales departments but by the scholar-teachers who are responsible for these volumes.

University of California,   *C. Warren Hollister*
Santa Barbara

CONTENTS

THE COMMUNE OF PARIS, 1871

INTRODUCTION

In presenting an anthology of readings, some editors endeavor to maintain a strict neutrality, leaving the matter of interpretation wholly to the readers. No reader, however, should be lulled into the innocence of believing in the possibility of neutrality; and, in this case, he is urged to recognize that the editor has a point of view about the Commune of Paris that differs in some way from every selection in the anthology. In the main those differences can be detected in the introductory remarks and may serve as a foil against which to examine the problems of interpretation in the book. No doubt even the choice of readings in the book reflect the editor's particular reconstruction of the historical events.

The selections in this short volume, indeed, have been chosen to illustrate both the passions and the interpretations of the Commune of Paris, for the former have always colored the latter. A revolutionary moment of great violence, the Commune was in fact part of a larger revolutionary pattern. And although it adds difficulties to an already difficult study, the reader will, in the long run, make more sense out of the Commune if he keeps in mind the larger context.

Toward the end of the Second Empire, that regime began its well-known drift to the Left that culminated on January 2, 1870, in the formation of the Liberal Empire, a limited monarchy. In the eighteenth century, an absolute government had not known how to reform itself and had, thus, suffered from a revolution. In the nineteenth century, the absolute monarch, Napoleon III, undertook to begin and to direct the revolution. Its progress was feared by both Left and Right: the Left because it feared that the Emperor's revolution would preserve both monarchy and a society based upon religious principles; the Right because it feared that the Emperor's revolution meant the gradual democratization of society. His revolution, however, had overwhelming popular support, and its progress was halted not by the Opposition but by the outbreak of the Franco-Prussian War in July, 1870, and the subsequent capture of Napoleon III at Sedan. Paris, which had been the center of Leftist opposition to the Empire, now became the focal point of new revolutionary activity. On September 4, 1870, the Parisian deputies in the Imperial *Corps législatif*, all Republican, seized the opportunity to declare the imperial regime overthrown and formed an emergency Government of National Defense dedicated to continuing the war until satisfactory peace terms could be reached with Prussia.

The Revolution had thus moved a step to the left, but only a step. The Republicans in power were liberal in economic and social philosophy and, hence, conservatives in the eyes of a variety of political groups in Paris who espoused more radical doctrines. The Government of National Defense was seriously handicapped from its beginning by having to turn defeat into victory, by naively expecting a quick peace with easy terms from Prussia, and by the fact that an embryo "government" was waiting in the wings, ready to seize power if the moderate Republicans should falter. This embryo "government," known as the Central Committee of the Twenty Arrondissements, professed to represent the twenty municipalities of Paris. Its instigators were men imbued with the ideas of Proudhon and affiliated with the International Association of Workingmen. That is, they were socialists who favored the advancement of liberty and economic well-being by decentralizing political power and by forming mutual-aid organizations. They were humane, nonviolent, antiauthoritarian, envisioning a France of federated, cooperating municipalities (*communes*) where private property would be permitted only insofar as it would not be used to exploit mankind.

These instigators almost immediately lost control of the Central Committee, which fell into the hand of Jacobins and Blanquists. The former were nonsocialist Republicans of the Robespierre tradition who stood for the highly centralized state and who favored the use of terror to gain political ends. Unlike the parliamentary Republicans then in power, the Jacobins believed in a dictatorship that would, as in 1792–1793, arm the people and drive back the invaders from the North. The Blanquists also derived from the great revolutionary tradition, but from that of Hébert and Babeuf; meaning that they, too, were centralizers, but that they were economic revolutionaries, more thoroughgoing egalitarians. They had a simple faith in the goodness of a society that would be communistic, but believed that such a society could only be achieved through violence and maintained by a dictatorship. The Blanquists, in short, advocated a centralized socialist state, whereas the Jacobins, like Robespierre, looked forward to the enforced perfectibility of man himself.

One thing that these various radicals could agree upon was the need to erect a new municipal government for Paris, namely the Paris Commune, which they realistically expected to dominate. The Government of National Defense had no intention of allowing such a rival government to be established in Paris, but also feared to hold national elections, which would have been an alternative. The rural masses had been supporting the Imperial regime, and the Republicans in power correctly suspected that rural votes might still be anti-Republican. Consequently, these Republicans soon found themselves in an impossible position: they dared not leave Paris, lacking a political base in the country, and therefore allowed themselves to become blockaded; this meant that they could not give adequate direction to armies still in the field. When military operations went sour and it became necessary to consider accepting the humiliating peace terms that Bismarck had offered, the Government also risked insurrection within Paris where the radicals argued that only they and their methods could save France from the "traitors" presumably about to deliver the country to the enemy. The news that Marshal Bazaine had surrendered Metz on October 27, 1870, was coupled with word of negotiations with Bismarck for an armistice. And the government now resolved at last to hold national elections so that there could be a national acceptance of the treaty terms that would follow. All this news infuriated the radicals, who marched on the Hôtel de Ville on October 31 and demanded that there be an end to negotiations and that the Government of National Defense give way to a Commune. The Government survived the insurrection only with difficulty, then failed to take effective measures against the leaders of the insurrection.

Meanwhile, those radical leaders had infiltrated a number of National Guard battalions whose officers were popularly elected. In consequence, the Government faced not merely increasing civil disorder but also the likelihood that many of its battalions were unreliable. Regular Army officers had little confidence in the "civilian" soldiers of the National Guard anyway and had been opposed to the mass sorties from the city that the radical leaders continually demanded. It happened that armistice negotiations between Bismarck and Jules Favre early in November broke down on various technicalities, but by the end of the year it had become clear in Paris that the fighting must cease and the city's suffering be brought to an end. With the resumption of negotiations on January 22 came a second insurrection by the radicals in their attempt to prevent peace and to establish a Commune. But this time the Government was ready, and the rebels were put to flight. An armistice was signed on January 28, which provided for national elections on February 8. By that date, the Republicans in general were regarded as the war party, for fighting to the bitter end. The country as a whole, wanting peace, therefore tended to vote against Republican candidates, while the city voters tended to stick with the Republicans as a matter of principle. This produced a great royalist majority in the new National Assembly at Bordeaux, just as it particularly separated Paris from the rest of the country in the Assembly. With the country seemingly bent upon peace at any price—for it was known that Bismarck demanded two provinces and a heavy indemnity—some of the radical leaders in Paris worked to make the National Guard even more political by federating its battalions under the leadership of a new Central Committee of the National Guard.

What was not always clear at the time, however, was that many in the National Guard favored such an organization for patriotic rather than political reasons. First, many simply believed that France could and must prevail in the war with Prussia. And second, it was never clear at the time, or later, just which radicals were members of the various organizations; for membership in the Central Committees constantly changed, and people outside Paris not only tended to lump the various radical organizations together in their minds as one vast conspiracy but were indifferent to the doctrinal differences that in fact divided the radicals. It made, and still makes, for enormous confusion about the development of the Commune.

The National Assembly now embarked upon settling the war,

taking steps that widened the rift between Paris and the country: it named Adolphe Thiers to be Chief of the Executive Power and retained the Republican form of government simply because the royalists were divided into three factions and could not for the moment agree upon a monarch. Since Thiers was generally regarded as a monarchist, his was thought to be merely a caretaker government He then presented the peace terms to the Assembly for ratification, which were reluctantly but overwhelming accepted after bitter denunciations from the Left. The Assembly then discussed the advisability of moving from Bordeaux to Paris but concluded that it was safer to remain outside the angry city. It chose Versailles instead on March 10, thus denying Paris her rightful "crown." Worse, the Assembly passed several laws that revealed either ignorance of, or indifference to, the economic and social conditions born of the long siege in Paris. The first was the Law of Maturities which ended the wartime moratorium on commercial paper and provided for the immediate collection of bills outstanding since the previous summer. A second measure ended the moratorium on rents, although the war had destroyed the livelihood of many of the city renters. Given the economic collapse of the city, such laws made no sense, and they drew Parisian workers and bourgeois together in outrage against the Assembly.

On March 11, 1871, the Assembly adjourned in order to move to Versailles, while Thiers moved the executive officers into Paris. He found the city in an ugly mood and quickly concluded that he must disarm its citizens. The attempt to remove large numbers of guns quietly during the night of March 18 was bungled by the Army, which instead set off wild public disorders and resulted in the assassination of two generals. Thiers at once removed his administration to Versailles, technically leaving governmental authority in the hands of the twenty mayors of the arrondissements, but in fact leaving the city a political vacuum.

The vacuum was filled by the Central Committee of the National Guard, somewhat dazed to find itself in power and anxious to relinquish it to a more regularly constituted political body. Despite the pleas of the more radical to use the opportunity to establish a dictatorship, a majority of the Central Committee insisted on democratic elections to provide a new municipal

council—the Commune of Paris. The mayors of the arrondissements strove to prevent such an act of defiance toward the
Assembly, but in vain. Paris and Versailles were drawing further
apart day by day. A crowd of pro-Assembly demonstrators in
the Place Vendôme had been fired upon by National Guards,
and ten of the demonstrators had been killed. The conflict was
now beyond the point of conciliation.

The Communal elections were held on schedule, March 26,
1871, and the voters returned a council that was overwhelmingly
revolutionary. A satisfactory analysis of the vote, however, has
never been possible. Available figures do not tell us how many
voters abstained nor what abstention meant. Even the act of
voting did not necessarily imply enthusiasm for a revolutionary
government. In short order, twenty-one of the ninety seats were
vacated by political moderates who refused to serve, and when
supplementary elections to fill vacated seats were held three
weeks later (April 16), the voter turnout was dismal.

From the start, the Council lacked any sort of homogeneity,
and its roster of ninety was never filled. We can identify approx-
imately thirty-four Jacobins on the Council, eleven Blanquists,
and perhaps twenty-five more who had had some prior affiliation
with the Proudhonian philosophy and the International Association of Workingmen. Other members defy classification. The
Jacobins and Blanquists, favoring dictatorship and terror, were
lumped together as the Majority. Those opposed to such methods
constituted the Minority. Only two of the members seem to have
had any real knowledge of German socialism and might properly
be called Marxian Communists. The remainder of the socialists
often did not faithfully follow any line or leader, making a
gelatin of the Minority. The political confusion was enriched
by the failure of the Central Committee of the National Guard
to wither away as promised after the elections. Its continual
proclamations came to be more radical than those of the Commune, no doubt misleading outsiders who could not distinguish
between the two bodies.

After the fighting began and the Versaillese commenced to
shoot prisoners, the Commune responded with a Law of Hostages,
providing for the arrest and trial of those thought to be pro-
Assembly. Under this law, the Public Prosecutor, Raoul Rigault,

directed most of his prosecutional efforts against priests, but the shooting of the hostages did not begin until the last days of the Commune. Otherwise, Communal legislation was surprisingly moderate. No attempt was made to seize the Bank of France, nor was private property confiscated. The matter of private debts was solved humanely by a decree of April 16 that gave debtors over three years to complete their payments and at no additional interest. Factionalism prevented the formulation of an official program for many days, and the myriad of necessary compromises resulted in a Declaration to the French People on April 19 that, in fact, represented Minority principles more than those of the Majority.

The military leadership of the Commune was equally inept and seriously handicapped by the suspicions born of political factionalism. As the Versaillese pressed in from the west, the political climate in the city became hysterical, permitting the Majority on May 1 to obtain sufficient support to establish a five-man dictatorship known as the Committee of Public Safety. From that moment on, the members of the Minority were in mortal danger. The final week of fighting May 21–28 was by far the worst, with hand-to-hand combat, both sides shooting prisoners, and the Communards setting fires for both defensive and revengeful reasons. The casualties have never been precisely known: probably 20,000 of the defenders fell, along with about 1000 of the attackers. Much of the slaughter was senseless—the simple working out of many months of national frustration and humiliation.

The Commune did not really end with the fighting. Legal reprisals continued for years, and the constitution of the Third Republic was far more conservative, as a reaction against the Commune, than one would have expected a French Republican constitution to be. Social legislation projected in the last years of the Second Empire was thereby delayed for decades, while the Parision voters were susceptible to extremist political causes that threatened the life of the Republic right down to the end of the century. The high price of human folly has rarely been better measured.

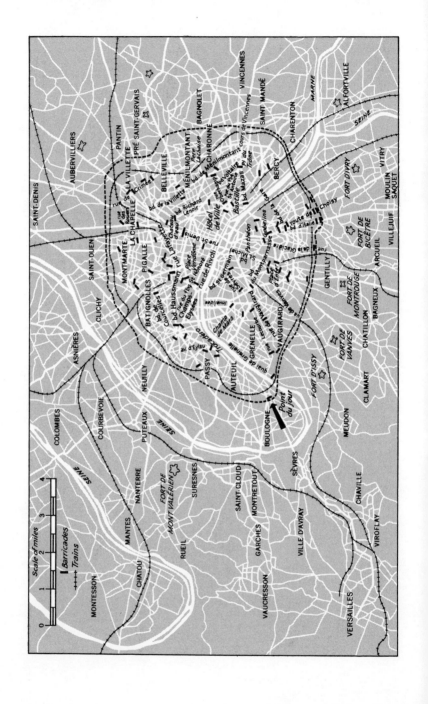

PART ONE

Eyewitness Accounts, Memoirs, and Histories
Representing Different Viewpoints

COMMUNARD

Prosper-Olivier Lissagaray

Prosper-Olivier Lissagaray (1839-1901) was a journalist who published several newspapers during the Second Empire in Paris and in his native Auch, suffering a number of condemnations for attacks upon the regime. After the Revolution of September 4, 1870, he became chef de cabinet *to the Minister of the Interior, Léon Gambetta. Unlike Gambetta, however, Lissagaray remained in Paris and gave his support to the Commune although never a member. He fled to London to escape certain prosecution, returning to France after the final amnesty was granted in 1880. Meanwhile, he had published his* History of the Commune of 1871, *history written by an eyewitness, passionately* procommunard, *which became something of a classic. The following extract reveals, even if one is unfamiliar with names and places, the tone of the volume as it portrays the heroism and the virtue of the Parisians.*

PARIS ON THE EVE OF DEATH

The Paris of the Commune has but three days more to live; let us engrave upon our memory her luminous physiognomy.

He who has breathed in thy life that fiery fever of contemporaneous history, who has panted on thy boulevards and wept in thy faubourgs, who has sung to the morns of thy revolutions and a few weeks after bathed his hands in powder behind thy bar-

SOURCE. Prosper-Olivier Lissagaray, *History of the Commune of 1871,* Eleanor Marx Aveling, tr., New York: International Publishers, 1898, pp. 293–303. Copyright 1898 by International Publishers.

ricades, he who can hear from beneath thy stones the voices of the martyrs of sublime ideas and read in every one of thy streets a date of human progress, even he does less justice to thy original grandeur than the stranger, though a Philistine, who came to glance at thee during the days of the Commune. The attraction of rebellious Paris was so strong that men hurried thither from America to behold this spectacle unprecedented in the world's history—the greatest town of the European continent in the hands of the proletarians. Even the pusillanimous were drawn towards her.

In the first days of May one of our friends arrived—one of the most timid men of the timid provinces. His kith and kin had escorted him on his departure, tears in their eyes, as though he were descending into the infernal regions. He said to us, "What is true in all the rumours bruited about?" "Well, come and search all the recesses of the den."

We set out from the Bastille. Street-arabs cry Rochefort's *Mot d'Ordre*, the *Pére Duchêne*, Jules Vallès' *Cri du Peuple*, Félix Pyat's *Vengeur*, *La Commune*, *L'Affranchi*, *Le Pilori des Mouchards*. The *Officiel* is little asked for; the journalists of the Council stifle it by their competition. The *Cri du Peuple* has a circulation of 100,000. It is the earliest out; it rises with chanticleer. If we have an article by Vallès this morning, we are in luck; but in his stead, Pierre Denis, with his autonomy *à outrance*, makes himself too often heard. Only buy the *Père Duchêne* once, though its circulation is more than 60,000. Take Félix Pyat's article in the *Vengeur* as a fine example of literary intoxication. The bourgeoisie has no better helpmates than these vain and ignorant claptrapmongers. Here is the doctrinaire journal *La Commune*, in which Millière sometimes writes, and in which Georges Duchêne takes the young men and the old of the Hôtel-de-Ville to task with a severity which would better fit another character than his. Do not forget the *Mot d'Ordre*, whatever the romanticists may say. It was one of the first to support the Revolution of the 18th March, and darted terrible arrows at the Versaillese.[1]

[1] Except for the *Officiel*, these are references to the best-known radical journals published in Paris during the Commune. Jules Vallès and Félix Pyat were both members of the Commune; Henri Rochefort and J. B. Millière were not. (Editor's note.)

In the kiosques are the caricatures. Thiers, Picard, and Jules Favre figure as the Three Graces, clasping each other's paunches. This fine fish, the *maquereau*, with the blue-green scales, who is making up a bed with an imperial crown, is the Marquis de Gallifet. *L'Avenir*, the mouthpiece of the *Ligue*. *Le Siècle*, become very hostile since the arrest of Gustave Chaudey; and *La Vérité*, the Yankee Portalis's paper, are piled up, melancholy and intact. Many reactionist papers have been suppressed by the prefecture, but for all that are not dead; for a lad, without any mystery about him, offers them to us.

Read, search, find one appeal to murder, to pillage, a single cruel line in all these Communard journals excited by the battle, and then compare them with the Versaillese papers, demanding fusillades *en masse* as soon as the troops shall have vanquished Paris.

Let us follow those catafalques that are being taken up the Rue de la Roquette, and enter with them into the Père Lachaise cemetery. All those who die for Paris are entombed with obsequies in the great resting-place. The Commune has claimed the honour of paying for their funerals; its red flag blazes from the four corners of the hearse, followed by some comrades of the battalion, while a few passers-by always join the procession. This is a wife accompanying her dead husband. A member of the Council follows the coffin; at the grave he speaks not of regrets, but of hope, of vengeance. The widow presses her children in her arms, and says to them, "Remember and cry with me, 'Vive la République! Vive la Commune!' "

On retracing our steps, we pass by the mairie of the eleventh arrondissement. It is hung with black, the mourning of the last Imperialist plébiscite, of which the people of Paris was innocent and became the victim. We cross the Place de la Bastille, gay, animated by the ginger-bread fair. Paris will yield nothing to the cannon; she has even prolonged the annual fair for a week. The swings move to and fro, the wheels-of-fortune turn, booth-keepers cry their sixpenny wares, the mountebanks allure spectators, and promise half their receipts to the wounded.

We go down these great boulevards. A crowd pushes against the Napoleon Circus, where 5,000 people are gathered, filling it from the area to the ceiling. Small flags, each one bearing the name of a department, urge the provincials to group themselves. This meeting has been called by some merchants, who propose to the citizens of the departments to send delegates to their respective deputies, in the belief that the latter may be brought round and peace gained by explanations. A tall, thin man, with a sad face, asks for permission to address the people, and gets upon the platform. It is Millière, whom the crowd cheers. "Peace," said he, "we all wish for it, citizens. But who, then, has commenced the war? Who attacked Paris on the 18th March? M. Thiers. Who attacked her on the 2nd April? M. Thiers. Who has spoken of conciliation, multiplied attempts at peace? Paris. Who has always repulsed them? M. Thiers. Conciliation! M. Dufaure has said, 'Why, insurrection is less criminal.' And that which neither the Freemasons, nor the leagues, nor the addresses, nor the municipal councillors of the provinces could do, you expect to get from a deputation chosen from amongst the Parisians! See, without knowing it, you are enervating the defence. No, no more deputations, but active correspondence with the provinces—there lies salvation!" "This, then, is that energumen whom we are so frightened of in the provinces!" exclaimed our friend. "Yes, and these thousands of men of all conditions, who in common seek for peace, consult each other, answer courteously, these are the demented people, the handful of bandits who hold the capital."

Before the Prince Eugène Barracks we notice the 1,500 soldiers who remained in Paris on the 18th March, and whom the Commune entertains without asking them for any service. At the top of the Boulevard Magenta we visit the numerous skeletons of the St. Laurent Church, arranged in the same order they were found in, without coffins or winding-sheets. Are not interments in churches formally prohibited, Some, however, Notre Dame des Victoires especially, abound in skeletons. Is it not the duty of the Commune to expose these illegal proceedings, which are perhaps crimes?

On the boulevards, from Bonne-Nouvelle to the Opéra, we find the same Paris loitering before the shops, sitting in front of the cafés. Carriages are rare, for the second siege has cut short the provisions for horses. By the Rue du 4 Septembre we reach the Stock Exchange, surmounted by the red flag, and the Bibliothèque Nationale, where readers are sitting round the long tables. Crossing the Palais-Royal, whose arcades are always noisy, we come to the Museum of the Louvre; the rooms, hung with their pictures, are open to the public. The Versaillese journals none the less say the Commune is selling the national collections to foreigners.

We descend the Rue de Rivoli. On the right, in the Rue Castiglione, a huge barricade obstructs the entrance of the Place Vendôme. The issue of the Place de la Concorde is barred by the St. Florentin redoubt, stretching to the Ministry of Marine on its right, and the garden of the Tuileries on its left, with three rather badly directed embrasures eight yards wide. An enormous ditch, laying bare all the arteries of subterranean life, separates the place from the redoubt. The workmen are giving it the finishing stroke, and cover the epaulments with gazon. Many promenaders look on inquisitively, and more than one brow lowers. A corridor skilfully constructed conducts us to the Place de la Concorde. The proud profile of the Strasbourg statue stands out against the red flags. The Communards, who are accused of ignoring France, have piously replaced the faded crowns of the first siege by fresh spring flowers.

We now enter the zone of battle. The avenue of the Champs-Elysées unrolls its long-deserted line, cut by the dismal bursting of the shells from Mont-Valérien and Courbevoie. These reach as far as the Palais de l'Industrie, whose treasures the employés of the Commune courageously protect. In the distance rises the mighty bulk of the Arc de Triomphe. The sightseers of the first days have disappeared, for the Place de l'Etoile has become almost as deadly as the rampart. The shells break off the bas-reliefs that M. Jules Simon had caused to be iron-clad against the Prussians. The main arch is walled up to stop the projectiles that enfiladed it. Behind this barricade they are getting ready to mount some pieces on the platform, which is almost as high as Mont-Valérien.

By the Faubourg St. Honoré we pass along the Champs-Elysées. In the right angle comprised between the Avenue de la Grande Armée, that of the Ternes, the ramparts, and the Avenue Wagram there is not a house intact. You see M. Thiers "does not bombard Paris, as the people of the Commune will not fail to say." Some shreds of a placard hang from a half-battered wall; it is M. Thiers' speech against King Bomba, which a group of conciliators have been witty enough to reproduce. "You know, gentlemen," said he to the bourgeois of 1848, "what is happening at Palermo. You all have shaken with horror on hearing that during forty-eight hours a large town has been bombarded. By whom? Was it by a foreign enemy exercising the rights of war? No, gentlemen, it was by its own Government. And why? Because that unfortunate town demanded its rights. Well, then, for the demand of its rights it has got forty-eight hours of bombardment!" Happy Palermo! Paris already has had forty days of bombardment.

We have some chance of getting to the Boulevard Péreire by the left side of the Avenue des Ternes. From there to the Porte-Maillot every spot is beset with danger. Watching for a momentary lull, we reach the gate, or rather the heap of ruins that mark its place. The station no longer exists, the tunnel is filled up, the ramparts are slipping into the moats. And yet there are human salamanders who dare to move about amidst these ruins. Facing the gate there are three pieces commanded by Captain La Marseillaise; on the right, Captain Rouchat with five pieces; on the left, Captain Martin with four. Monteret, who commands this post for the last five weeks, lives with them in this atmosphere of shells. The Mont-Valérien, Courbevoie, and Bécon have thrown more than eight hundred of them. Twelve pieces are served by ten men, naked to the waist, their body and arms blackened with powder, in a stream of perspiration, often a match in each hand. The only survivor of the first set, the sailor Bonaventure, has twenty times seen his comrades dashed to pieces. And yet they hold out, and these pieces, continually dismounted, are continually renewed; their artillerists only complain of the want of munition, for the waggons no longer dare approach. The Versaillese have very often attempted, and may attempt, surprises. Monteret watches day and night, and he can without boasting write to the Committee of Public Safety that so long as he is there the Versaillese will not enter by the Porte-Maillot.

Every step towards La Muette is a challenge to death. But our friend must witness all the greatness of Paris. On the ramparts, near the gate of La Muette, an officer is waving his képi toward the Bois de Boulogne; the balls are whistling around him. It is Dombrowski,[2] who is amusing himself with inveighing against the Versaillese of the trenches. A member of the Council who is with him succeeds in making him forego this musketeer fool-hardiness, and the general takes us to the castle, where he has established one of his headquarters. All the rooms are perforated by shells. Still he remains there, and makes his men remain. It has been calculated that his aides-de-camp on an average lived eight days. At this moment the watch of the Belvedere rushes in with appalled countenance; a shell has traversed his post. "Stay there," says Dombrowski to him; "If you are not destined to die there you have nothing to fear." Such was his courage—all fatalism. He received no reinforcements despite his despatches to the War office; believed the game lost, and said so but too often.

This is my only reproach, for you do not expect me to apologise for the Commune's having allowed foreigners to die for it. Is not this the revolution of all proletarians? Is it not for the people to at last do justice to that great Polish race which all French governments have betrayed?

Dombrowski accompanies us across Passy as far as the Seine, and shows us the almost abandoned ramparts. The shells crush or mow down all the approaches to the railway; the large viaduct is giving way at a hundred places; the iron-clad locomotives have been overthrown. The Versaillese battery of the Billancourt Isle fires point-blank at our gunboats, and sinks one, *L'Estoc*, under our very eyes. A tug arrives in time, picks up the crew, and ascends the Seine under the fire that follows it up to the Jena Bridge.

A clear sky, a bright sun, peaceful silence envelop this stream, this wreck, these scattered shells. Death appears more cruel amidst the serenity of nature. Let us go and salute our wounded at Passy. A member of the Council, Lefrançais,[3] is visiting the ambulance of Dr. Demarquay, whom he questions as to the state of the wounded. "I do not share your opinions," answers the

[2] Jaroslaw Dombrowski, a Polish refugee soldier, was Commander-in-Chief for a few days in May. He was later killed in the final assault upon Paris. (Editor's note.)

[3] Gustave Lefrançais: see the next selection. (Editor's note.)

doctor, "and I cannot desire the triumph of your cause; but I have never seen wounded men preserve more calm and sang-froid during operations. I attribute this courage to the energy of their convictions." We then visit the beds; most of the sick anxiously inquire when they will be able to resume their service. A young fellow of eighteen, whose right hand had just been amputated, holds out the other, exclaiming, "I have still this one for the service of the Commune!" An officer, mortally wounded, is told that the Commune has just handed over his pay to his wife and children. "I had no right to it," answers he. "These, my friend, these are the brutish drunkards who, according to Versailles, form the army of the Commune."

We return by the Champ-de-Mars; its huts are badly manned. Other *cadres*, a different discipline would be needed to retain the battalions there. Before the Ecole, 1500 yards from the ramparts, and a few steps from the War Office, a hundred ordnance pieces remain inert, loaded with mud. Leaving on our right the War Office, that centre of discord, let us enter the Corps Législatif, transformed into a workshop. Fifteen hundred women are there, sewing the sand sacks that are to stop the breaches. A tall and handsome girl, Marthe, round her waist the red scarf with silver fringe given her by her comrades, distributes the work. The hours of labour are shortened by joyous songs. Every evening the wages are paid, and the women receive the whole sum, eight centimes a sack, while the former contractors hardly gave them two.

We now proceed along the quays, lulled in imperturbable calm. The Academy of Sciences holds its Monday sittings. It is not the workmen who have said, "The Republic wants no savants." M. Delaunay is in the chair. M. Elie de Beaumont looks through the correspondence, and reads a note from his colleague, M. J. Bertrand, who has fled to St. Germain. We shall find the report in the *Officiel* of the Commune.

We must not leave the left bank without visiting the military prison. Ask the soldiers if they have met with a single menace, a single insult in Paris; if they are not treated as comrades, subjected to no exceptional rules, set free when willing to help their Parisian brothers.

Meanwhile evening has set in. The theatres are opening. The

Lyrique gives a grand performance for the benefit of the
wounded, and the Opéra-Comique is preparing another. The
Opéra promises us a special performance for the following Monday, when we shall hear Gossec's revolutionary hymn. The
artists of the Gaieté, abandoned by their manager, themselves
direct their theatre. The Gymnase, Châtelet, Théâtre-Français,
Ambigu-Comique, Délassements, have large audiences every night.
Let us pass to more virile spectacles, such as Paris has not witnessed since 1793.

Ten churches open, and the Revolution mounts the pulpits.
In the old quarter of the Gravilliers, St. Nicholas des Champs is
filling with the powerful murmur of many voices. A few gas-
burners hardly light up the swarming crowd; and at the farther
end, almost hidden by the shadow of the vaults, hangs the figure
of Christ draped in the popular oriflamme. The only luminous
centre is the reading-desk, facing the pulpit, hung with red. The
organ and the people chant the *Marseillaise*. The orator, over-
excited by these fantastic surroundings, launches forth into ec-
static apostrophes, which the echo repeats like a menace. The
people discuss the events of the day, the means of defence; the
members of the Council are severely censured, and vigorous
resolutions are voted to be presented to the Hôtel-de-Ville the
next day. Women sometimes ask to speak; at the Batignolles they
have a club of their own. No doubt, few precise ideas come forth
from these feverish meetings, but many find there a provision
of energy and of courage.

It is only nine o'clock, and we may still be in time for the
concert of the Tuileries. At the entrance, citoyennes, accompanied by commissioners, are making a collection for the widows
and orphans of the Commune. The immense rooms are animated
by a decent and gay throng. For the first time respectably-dressed
women are seated on the forms of the court. Three orchestras
are playing in the galleries, but the soul of the fête is in the Salle
des Maréchaux, where Mademoiselle Agar recites from "Les
Châtiments" in that same place, where, ten months before, Bonaparte and his band were enthroned. Mozart, Meyerbeer, Rossini,
the great works of art have driven away the musical obscenities
of the Empire. From the large central window the harmonious
strains vibrate to the garden; joyous lights shine like stars on

the green-sward, dance among the trees, and colour the playing fountains. Within the arbours the people are laughing; but the noble Champs-Elysées, dark and desolate, seem to protest against these popular masters, whom they have never acknowledged. Versailles, too, protests by that conflagration of which a wan reflex lights up the Arc de Triomphe, whose sombre mass over-towers the civil war.

At eleven o'clock, as the crowd is retiring, we hear a noise from the side of the chapel. M. Schœlcher has just been arrested. He has been taken to the prefecture, where, a few hours after, the procureur Rigault sets him at liberty.[4]

The boulevards are thronged with the people coming from the theatres. At the Café-Peters there is a scandalous gathering of staff-officers and prostitutes. Suddenly a detachment of National Guards appears and leads them off. We follow them to the Hôtel-de-Ville, where Ranvier, who is on duty there, receives them.[5] Short shrift is made: the women to St. Lazare, the officers, with spades and mattocks, to the trenches.

One o'clock in the morning. Paris sleeps tranquilly. Such, my friend, is the Paris of the brigand. You have seen this Paris thinking, weeping, combating, working, enthusiastic, fraternal, severe to vice. Her streets free during the day, are they less safe in the silence of the night? Since Paris has her own police crime has disappeared. Each one is left to his instincts, and where do you see debauchery victorious? These Federals, who might draw milliards, live on ridiculous pay compared with their usual salaries. Do you at last recognize this Paris, seven times shot down since 1789, and always ready to rise for the salvation of France? Where is her programme, say you? Why, seek it before you, and not at the faltering Hôtel-de-Ville. These smoking ramparts, these explosions of heroism, these women, these men of all professions united, all the workmen of the earth applauding our combat, all

[4] Victor Schoelcher, a Republican journalist, was one of the deputies from Paris who tried to prevent the outbreak of civil war. It is believed that he owed his above liberty to a promise to give up seeking reconciliation. Raoul Rigault, a Blanquist, was the prosecuting attorney for the Commune. (Editor's note.)

[5] The Blanquist Gabriel Ranvier was a member of the Committee of Public Safety. (Editor's note.)

monarchs, all the bourgeois coalesced against us, do they not speak loudly enough our common thought, and that all of us are fighting for equality, the enfranchisement of labour, the advent of a social society? Woe to France if she does not comprehend! Leave at once; recount what Paris is. If she dies, what life remains to you? Who, save Paris, will have strength enough to continue the Revolution? Who save Paris will stifle the clerical monster? Go, tell the Republican provinces, "These proletarians fight for you too, who perhaps may be the exiles of to-morrow." As to that class, the purveyor of empires, that fancies it can govern by periodical butcheries, go and tell them, in accents loud enough to drown their clamours, "The blood of the people will enrich the revolutionary field. The idea of Paris will arise from her burning entrails and become an inexorable firebrand with the sons of the slaughtered."

2   *Gustave Lefrançais*

Gustave Lefrançais (1826-1901) was a primary school teacher whose radical views cost him his position in 1850. Afterward an accountant, he spoke out frequently for collective ownership of property, against the inheritance of property, for free love, and against the institution of marriage. Too radical to side with the Moderate Republicans after the Revolution of September 4, 1870, he took part in the Insurrection of October 31. He was elected to the Commune from the Fourth Arrondissement and was given important committee assignments. As the following extract from a speech in the Commune shows, he voted with the Minority against the creation of a dictatorship. At the end of the Commune, he escaped to London and was condemned to death in absentia. The extract illustrates not only the disunity

SOURCE. *Procès-verbaux de la Commune*, Session of May 19, 1871. Translated for this book by Roger L. Williams. Copyright 1959 by Editions sociales (Paris) in Arthur Adamov, *La Commune de Paris*. Original reference is to manuscript in the Musée Carnavalet in Paris.

within the Commune but the democratic principles of the Minority, many of whom were Proudhonians. Lefrançais was known to have been affiliated with the International.

When the Commune emerged triumphant from the events so courageously managed by the Central Committee [of the National Guard] on March 18, certain members of the Commune thought that at long last those principles that they had advanced on the previous October 31 were now going to be realized. The main principle that had guided them was this: that the Commune ought to be the executive agent of the public will, representing that will at all times and taking the lead to show what must be done to guarantee that the Revolution will prevail. Conceiving of the Commune in such terms ultimately led to the formation of a Minority within the Commune. . . . At a given point, the Commune of Paris deemed it necessary to centralize the operation [of government] by establishing an inner group, a special machinery, called the Committee of Public Safety. The Minority objected to its creation for two reasons: (1) because [the Minority] had been guided from the beginning by the premise that the sovereign power resides in the voters of Paris as a whole, the Commune being only the executive agent of that power; and that in the light of that principle, the members of the Commune have received no sanction from the voters to appropriate that sovereignty belonging only to the voters; and (2) because the Minority regarded the historical precedent [for such a committee] to have had unfortunate aspects. The Majority, indeed, seems not to have been sufficiently mindful of the fact that the Committee of Public Safety of '93 was the antagonist of the Commune, an agency of the Convention, the born enemy of the Commune, and its executioner. . . . We must remember that the fall of that Commune of Paris was the deathblow to the French Revolution, which fell stricken on the ninth Thermidor. Such were the fatal consequences of that Committee of Public Safety, it, too, instituted to save the Revolution. Prompted by these historical memories, the Minority rejected the creation of a special body that seemed likely to jeopardize the sovereignty of the Commune. I can only hope that the future will prove that we were wrong. Meanwhile, our convictions cannot be set aside and, in view of those convictions, we have protested against the creation of the Committee of Public Safety.

3   *Charles Amouroux*

Charles Amouroux (1848-1885), a provincial hat maker who moved to Paris during the Second Empire and soon took an active part in labor politics, becoming known as a violent opponent of the established social order. Jailed in 1869, he fled abroad in 1870 to escape further imprisonment, associating with political refugees and with members of the International. After the Revolution of September 4, he joined the French Army, but opposed the moderates in the Government of National Defense. He was elected to the Commune by the Fourth Arrondissement and became Secretary to the Commune. As this extract shows, he voted for the Committee of Public Safety. Amouroux was neither a Jacobin nor a Blanquist in affiliation, yet was known as one of the most violent personalities in the Commune. He was one of the few members caught by the Versailles and was condemned to forced labor for life. After the amnesty, he was elected to be deputy from the Loire. Here he answers Lefrançais's opposition to the Committee of Public Safety.

You are told about a schism between the Majority and the Minority. When the Commune was established, I did not think that such a thing as a majority or a minority could exist. I believed that we had a common goal, and that if on certain matters we were not always in agreement, we had to be [in agreement] on fundamentals. But there have been different points of view. Some have maintained that it would be improper to return to '93,

SOURCE. *Procès-verbaux de la Commune*, Session of May 19, 1871. Translated for this book by Roger L. Williams. Copyright 1959 by Editions sociales (Paris) in Arthur Adamov, *La Commune de Paris*. Original reference is to manuscript in the Musée Carnavalet in Paris.

that we must become socialists or intellectuals and choose reason rather than force. As for me, I have believed from the start that any revolution, born of force, can sustain itself only through the use of force. It is quite true that the socialist principle, emanating as it does from notions of right and justice, can only benefit from reasoning; but do we really have the right at this time to concern ourselves with social principles when we find ourselves opposed by men who are executing those of us taken prisoner?

Some of my colleagues have criticized me for attending meetings of the [popular] clubs. . . . The real strength of the Assembly, however, depends upon its awareness of the demands of the population. I have felt that the Commune has not been making good on its promises to the voters, that the Commune has been too lenient, and that it has not been sufficiently severe. I speak rarely in the Commune, but whenever I have spoken I have always been critical of the Commune for not being sufficiently revolutionary. When the Versaillese began murdering prisoners, we talked of energetic countermeasures. Versailles then halted the executions for a time but, as the Commune did not implement its [Law of Hostages], the Versaillese resumed the executions. It was at that point that we believed it had become necessary to form a Committee of Public Safety. . . . This Committee of Public Safety has been created in order that the members of the Commune may continue to meet while the Committee of Public Safety enacts the most energetic measures. . . . If the Reactionaries are not to triumph, the Commune must take the most decisive measures. It will be said to us, "Are you not afraid of shedding blood? Do you not fear to execute some hostages?" And I shall reply: "Did the Versaillese so reflect when they took prisoners and assassinated them?" Let us not be hesitant, but rather answer assassinations with some executions. (Applause.)

Some say that this is murder. But how can you use such a word when it is the people who are so acting, those who for eighteen centuries have been the murdered ones? When [the people] execute those who have been murdering them for eighteen centuries, can you call such executions murder? (Prolonged applause.)

Citizens! Let us show this assembly sitting in Versailles that

we are citizens who are fighting for right and for justice, but
that when one of ours is murdered, we know how to respond
with frightful executions. In so acting, we should be preventing
the spilling of blood; for while the Commune has been inactive,
more than 500 prisoners have been murdered. Faced with such
facts, do you mean to set up tribunals? Were there any along the
roads between Paris and Versailles? (Sensation.) . . .

   We are a revolutionary people. Yet, since 1793 and 1794 we
have been completely crushed. Today we are emancipating ourselves, and we must do it in a manner so complete that no more
18th Brumaires will be possible; for a people can be saved only
by themselves. It is precisely for that reason that the Committee
of Public Safety has been established: in order to take the most
energetic measures, and in order that various members of the
Commune may go to the battlefields. At the same time, we have
proposed that there be two sessions per week so that the Commune may judge the activities of the Committee and even destroy
the Committee if it be deemed necessary. . . .

REPUBLICAN

4   *Ludovic Halévy*

*Ludovic Halévy (1834-1908) was a member of a French-Jewish
family that has been prominent in French intellectual and literary
affairs for over a century. He was most successful as a librettist,
especially for Offenbach* (La Belle Hélène, La Grande Duchesse de
Gérolstein, *and* La Périchole), *but he also held minor government
posts, thanks to the patronage of the Duc de Morny during the
Second Empire. Halévy is hard to classify, possessing ambivalent
political and social attitudes. He had characteristics of both liberal
Bonapartism and conservative Republicanism; yet his attitudes were
probably motivated more by literary and artistic standards than by
political or social concern. He left several volumes of insightful
memoirs, from one of which this extract is drawn,[1] showing the
impact of burning Paris upon the sensitive, middle-ground observer.*

Before returning to Versailles, we wanted to make a tour of
the fires. . . . This morning, on leaving Versailles [for Paris], our
friend Joseph Bertrand, permanent secretary to the Academy of
Sciences, said to us, "Bring me back news of my house."

We first took the rue Montmartre: a great crowd near Les
Halles [the central market] outside [the church of] Saint-
Eustache; a shell from Père-Lachaise had just fallen there five

[1] Halévy's tour evidently took place either May 27 or 28, 1871. (Editor's
note.)

SOURCE. Ludovic Halévy, *Notes et souvenirs*, Second edition, Paris: Calmann-Lévy, 1889, pp. 69–73. Translated for this book by Roger L. Williams.
Copyright 1889 by Calmann-Lévy.

minutes before, but had not exploded or done any harm. We proceed to M. Bertrand's house. Nothing more than four walls around a heap of still-smoking rubbish. Bertrand has lost everything: his papers, his books, his manuscripts, his notes, thirty years of work and study—all that is under these ruins. We saw M. Bertrand again that evening in Versailles. He got this frightful news, and never has such great misfortune been endured with such heroic simplicity. It is all to be done over; he will begin again.

Here we are before the Hôtel de Ville. What a frightful, yet wonderful, ruin! These walls, ripped and burned by fire, ought to be left as they are, forever, in the very heart of Paris, as an eternal lesson, as witness to our mistakes, our disagreements, our follies.

On the interior the great woodwork still burns and smokes. All around the square are great barricades, smashed and gutted. An enclosure of planks surrounds the Hôtel de Ville, on one of the boards a placard partially consumed by the fire. It is the last proclamation of the Commune bearing the number 395. Three hundred and ninety-five proclamations in two months! *The Commune to the Versaillese soldiers. Brothers, the moment of the great struggle of peoples against their oppressors has come. Do not abandon the cause of the workers, etc.*

With infinite care—nothing stops a collector—I succeed in removing this placard and carry it off as a souvenir of this tragic tour. Moving on, we cross the Pont-Neuf and come upon a large fire. It is a large dry-goods store that has been aflame for forty-eight hours. Next to it the stores are open, the passers-by are numerous, active, bustling about, businesslike, having resumed the brisk demeanor of the Parisian; the neighboring streets have recovered their activity, their character, their usual appearance. For five minutes I stop and watch with fascination an optician in the rue du Vieux-Colombier, who, with great deliberation, is busy rearranging his showcase. He systematically places his opera glasses, his glasses, his binoculars, and microscopes. His wife gives advice; he comes out of the shop *to see the effect* of his window from the sidewalk, while the fire rages on a hundred yards from there, and artillery fires in the direction of the Bastille can be clearly heard.

During this rapid trip across Paris, in the midst of destruction and fire, while fighting rages on around Père-Lachaise, certainly what has astonished me the most is this immediate resumption of life in this great human ant hill. Following the victorious Versailles troops, life suddenly emerges on the pavement. Yes, they are really ants, coming out of their holes to search about and to rediscover, after this great upheaval, their routes and habits of yesterday.

We start walking along the quaies, breathing an acrid air that is sickening. Beginning at the Pont-Royal, we enter a real hedge of fires: at the Tuileries, in the rue du Bac, at the State Deposit and Consignment Bank, at the Council of State, and in the Palace of the Legion of Honor. This work has been done deliberately and by people who knew what they were doing.

During the past ten months I have witnessed many extraordinary things, but nothing stranger nor more fantastic than what I saw there in a short time with my own two eyes. Between the Pont-Royal and the Pont de la Concorde, I counted twelve fishermen at their ease, absolutely indifferent to what was going on above their heads, eyes glued to the little bobbers that fidgeted at the end of their lines, taking advantage of all these disasters *to fish out of season.*

We got back into our carriage . . . and were back in Versailles in an hour and a half. What a day!

5   *Emile Zola*

Emile Zola (1840-1902) was both a Republican journalist and a great novelist in the documentary tradition of Naturalism. As a newspaper reporter, he covered the sessions of the National Assembly in Bordeaux and then in Versailles, increasingly heartsick at the divisions in Republican ranks that the Commune was making, fearful that they would make a royalist restoration possible. As this brief extract shows,[1]

[1] Probably his walk took place on May 29 or 30, 1871. (Editor's note.)

SOURCE. Le Sémaphore, May 31, 1871. Translated for this book by Roger L. Williams. Copyright 1959 by Editions sociales, reprinting from le Sémaphore, May 31, 1871.

Zola was humane and compassionate, outraged by injustice and violence, and his literary life amounted to a long protest against social evil.

I have just completed a walk through Paris. It is dreadful! I mean to speak to you only about the heaps of bodies that have been piled up under the bridges. Never, never shall I forget the frightful seizure I experienced when faced with that mass of bleeding human flesh, dumped at random at the collection points. Heads and limbs are jumbled in grotesque dismemberment. From the piles, convulsed faces emerge, feet stick out. Some of the dead seem to be cut in two, while others seem to have four legs and four arms. What a lugubrious charnel house!

6 *Edmond de Goncourt*

Edmond de Goncourt (1822-1896) was the elder brother of the fraternal partnership that in a period of twenty years produced over thirty volumes of history, plays, novels, art criticism, and their most splendid work, a diary. Jules, the younger brother, died mid-1870, after which Edmond alone continued the diary. Though aristocratic, fastidious men, the Goncourts were of the Naturalist school, believing that in a democratic century the lives of the lower classes ought to be the proper subjects of literary inquiry, and that the scientific method ought to be the writer's method. Thus, Edmond was a conscientious observer of the social scene, as this extract from the diary reveals, and the picture he gives us of the last days of the Commune is both documentary and artistic.

SOURCE. Edmond de Goncourt, *Journal des Goncourts*, Paris: Charpentier, 1903, Vol. IV, pp. 322-329. Translated for this book by Roger L. Williams. Copyright 1903 by Bibliothèque-Charpentier.

Friday, May 26 [1871]. I was walking along the railway near the Passy station, when I saw some men and women surrounded by soldiers.

I cleared a damaged barrier and found myself at the edge of the road on which the prisoners were about to leave for Versailles. They were quite numerous, for I heard an officer say in a low voice as he handed a paper to the colonel, "407, of whom 66 are women."

The men had been divided into groups of eight and tied to one another with cord, wrist to wrist. There they were, evidently taken by surprise, most of them without hats, without caps, hair plastered to foreheads and faces by a fine rain that had been falling all morning. Some of them had made a head covering of their blue bandanas. Others, soaked with rain, clutch a thin topcoat across their chests which bulge from chunks of bread. It is a company of all kinds, tough-looking workers, artisans wearing jerseys, middle-class people wearing socialist ornaments, National Guardsmen who had not had time to shed their military trousers, two infantrymen [deserters] with a deathly pallor; faces that are stupid, ferocious, bored, and blank.

The same cross section is evident among the women. Next to the woman wearing a kerchief is a woman in a silk dress. One glimpses middle-class women, working-class women, and mere girls, one of the latter dressed in National Guard uniform. In the midst of all these faces, the bestial head of a poor creature stands out, a bruise covering half her face. None of these woman reveal the apathy characteristic of the men. Anger is on their faces, and contempt. Many have a gleam of madness in their eyes.

Among the women there is an outstandingly handsome one with the stern beauty of a young Fate. She is dark-skinned with frizzled, swept-up hair, eyes of steel, cheeks reddened by dried tears. She is a Pietà in a defiant pose, heaping abuse upon officers and soldiers alike, insults that pass through lips and in a voice so tightened by fury that they emerge as noises rather than words . . . and cannot be understood. "She's like the one who killed Barbier with a knife," a young officer says to one of his friends.

The least courageous of the women reveal their weakness only by hanging their heads slightly to the side, as do women who have been praying a long time in church. One or two veiled

their faces until a noncommissioned officer pushed aside one of
the veils with his riding crop, saying, "All right, take off those
veils and show your sluttish faces!"

The rain gets heavier. Some of the women pull skirts over
their heads. A row of cavalry in white cloaks has reinforced
the line of infantrymen. The colonel, one of those olive-hued
types, gives the order to be on the ready, and the African chasseurs load their carbines. This makes the women think that they
are going to be shot, and one of them becomes hysterical. But
the terror lasts only a moment, and almost immediately they
resume their contemptuous faces, a few even flirting with the
soldiers.

The chasseurs have slung their loaded carbines on their backs
and have drawn their sabers. The colonel now on the flank of
the column, yelling with a brutality that I sense is overdone to
engender fear, announces: "Death for any man who breaks away
from his neighbor's arm!" And this frightful "it means death"
is repeated four or five times in his short speech, during which
can also be heard the crisp noises of guns being loaded by the
foot soldiers.

All is ready for the departure, when the pity that never entirely
abandons mankind moves several of the foot soldiers to pass their
water bottles among the women. . . . The signal to move out is
then given, and the wretched column staggers off towards Versailles under the collapsing sky. . . .

Sunday, May 28. I am riding in the Champs Élysées in my
carriage. In the distance I see legs and more legs running in the
direction of the great avenue. I lean out of the carriage door. The
street is filled with an obscure mob hemmed in by two columns
of mounted troopers. I immediately get out and join the running
people. These are prisoners who have just been taken at the
Chaumont heights and who are being marched along five abreast,
a few women amongst them. One of the escorting horsemen
tells me that "there are six thousand here; five hundred were
shot [upon capture]."

Despite the horror one has for these people, the spectacle of
this dismal parade is afflicting. An occasional deserter can be
seen [among the prisoners], their coats turned inside out, gray

cloth pockets dangling around them, seemingly already half-undressed for the firing squad.

I meet Burty at the Madeleine. We start walking down the streets and on the boulevards, suddenly flooded with people emerging from their cellars and their hiding places. Unexpectedly meeting Mme. [Paul] Verlaine, Burty talks to her about ways of having her husband concealed; while Mme. Burty tells me a secret that her husband had kept from me. One of Burty's friends associated with the Committee of Public Safety had told him three or four days before the entry of the troops that the [Commune] government was no longer in control of anything, and that it was time to go into houses, empty them of furniture, and shoot the property owners.

I move on to the discovery of Paris burned! The Palais-Royal has been burned, but the attractive pediments on its two pavilions are still intact. The Tuileries will have to be rebuilt along the gardens and along the rue de Rivoli. . . . In places there are still traces and horrifying remains of the fighting. Here a dead horse, there near the stones of a half-demolished barricade some military caps bathing in a pool of blood. . . . I come to the Hôtel de Ville. The ruin is magnificent, splendid, beyond imagination: a ruin with the colors of sapphire, of rubies, of emeralds, dazzling like agates where kerosene has burned the stone, resembling a magic palace in an opera lighted by Bengal fires, . . . a graphic marvel to be preserved if the country were not condemned beyond appeal to the restorations of Viollet-le-Duc. Amidst the destruction of the buildings, a marble plaque shines intact, its deceitful device newly gilded. *Liberty, Equality, Fraternity.*

Suddenly I see the crowd begin to run. like an electrified crowd on a day of rioting. Then troopers appear, threatening, sabers in hand, making their horses rear, their kicks throwing passers-by from the street to the sidewalks. In their midst, a group of men are walking, at their head a man with a black beard, his forehead bandaged with a handkerchief. I noticed another man, being supported by his two neighbors as if he had not the strength to walk. These men have an unusual pallor with a dazed look that is etched on my mind.

I hear a woman cry out as she gets out of the way, "What bad luck to have come this way!" At my side, a calm bourgeois is counting one, two, three, — — — —. There are twenty-six of them. The escort is making these men run to the Lobau barracks where the gate closes after their entry. . . . I still do not understand but am seized by an indefinable anxiety. My bourgeois, who had just done the counting, then says to his neighbor:

"It will not be long now, you will soon hear the first rolling [of rifle fire]."

"What rolling?"

"Well, they're going to shoot them!"

Almost at once came an explosion, like an extraordinary noise enclosed within walls, a fusillade having the mechanical quality of a machine gun. A first, a second, a third, a fourth, a fifth murderous *rrara*—then a long pause—then a sixth, and still two more.

The noise seemed never to end. Finally it was quiet. The tenseness subsided, everyone began to breathe again, when there was a sharp crack, . . . then a second one, and finally the last. I am told that they are the *coups de grâce* administered by a policeman to those who are not dead.

At that moment, the execution platoon comes out of the door like a troop of drunks, blood on the ends of some of their bayonets. And while two closed baggage wagons go into the courtyard, out slips an ecclesiastic. . . .

VERSAILLESE

7   *Maxime Du Camp*

Maxime Du Camp (1822-1894) was both a journalist and a novelist. For many years he was a close friend of Flaubert, although the relationship became more formal during the Second Empire when Du Camp devoted himself increasingly to journalism and less to "pure" literature. A Romantic of sorts in his opposition to the bourgeois spirit, Du Camp nevertheless fought in the National Guard in June of 1848 for the established order. Yet, in 1860, he joined Garibaldi's band in Sicily. Beginning in 1867 he began publishing articles about Paris that ultimately became a six-volume work, Paris, ses organes, ses fonctions et sa vie dans la seconde moitié du XIXe siècle, *a masterpiece of reporting that also marked Du Camp's departure from Romanticism in favor of contemporary reality. Its sequel was a lengthy study of the Commune, from which this extract is taken, that was completed in 1879 and led to his election to the Académie française in 1880. The work well reflects Conservative Republican hostility to the Communards in the 1870's.*

The insurgents of 1871, who were driven by motives beyond accepted morality and were unconcerned for patriotism, who revolted against constituted authority and won an iniquitous victory, bringing into power slick and cruel windbags, tried to destroy a Paris they could no longer control. When brought before courts-martial, they showed neither quality nor strength;

SOURCE. Maxime Du Camp, *Les Convulsions de Paris*, fifth edition, Paris: Hachette, 1881, Vol. IV, pp. 320–331. Translated for this book by Roger L. Williams. Copyright 1880 by Librairie Hachette.

and in their meetings in exile, they have reasserted all variety of
nonsense that proves both their violence and their ineptitude.
There is not one of them who has not been seized by the demon
pride and who does not think himself cut out to build a model
civilization. Their arrogance is extreme; they think of themselves
as Christopher Columbuses embarked on the discovery of the
new world. They are so certain of seeing it emerge one day
from the fog of their delirium that they have already given it a
name, the Fourth Estate, . . . a social crucible of unprecedented
strength into which all the castes in French society will be
absorbed, mixed, and melted down. These men whose work we
have judged, for whom kerosene has been the final argument
and massacre the last word in reason, regard themselves as in-
novators, as prophets and saints, as the Gods in Genesis to whom
humanity comes in order to find its definitive form. They have
no regrets for what they have done. They have been soldiers of
Righteousness; and tomorrow, if they could, they would be the
executors of Justice. They hold their heads high, showing their
fists to civilization, boasting that they have given [civilization]
the rudest jolt it has ever sustained. . . .

They demand that the Fourth Estate be instituted, and that
all the privileges from which they have suffered be destroyed;
for they have discovered that contemporary society is founded
upon privilege. . . . They fight the wars of Hébert's and Marat's
day, repeating words that no longer make any sense and which
they have never understood. [They see] our society divided into
distinct classes: nobility, clergy, bourgeoisie, as in the time when
the *cahiers* for the Estates-General were drawn up, each class
armed with privileges with which it oppresses the people. [In
reality], the privileges of the nobility amount to the freedom to
go into business in order to subsist; there are dukes and counts
who are wine merchants. Clerical privileges allow the clergy
to wear cassocks with holes in the elbows, to be insulted without
answering back, to rescue, rear, and teach the children of people
who have shot down clergymen, priests whose dying act was
to bless their murderers. Bourgeois privilege means the right
to emerge from the masses through intelligence, hard work,
honesty, and thrift, as well as the right to fall back again through
ignorance, laziness, drunkenness, or waste. The privileges of

the people are not mentioned, but they are those that belong to every Frenchman: every career—every opportunity to rise —is open to all. More than one of our division commanders started out with rifle on shoulder; one of our greatest intellectuals began as a shoemaker; one of our fine writers was a cooper; and if I leaf through the biographical lists for the Institute, the National Assembly, the Senate, and the Civil Service, how many distinguished and respected men there are who ran barefooted in their childhood or who worked desperately hard in their early years! . . . A former worker, become an employer and now the mayor of one of the Parisian arrondissements, has written: "For the more than twenty years that we have lived among the working classes, we have noticed that all 'good' workers who have opened a business have done well."[1]

The privileges that the Fourth Estate means to eliminate exist only in the imagination of revolutionaries. One speaks of them, a great fuss is made about them; but they disappear when one tries to find them. This nonsense masks an assumption that must be exposed in simple terms: the Fourth Estate signifies that government ought to belong, by right of birth, to those who learn nothing, know nothing, and want to do nothing. It is an upside-down caste system. The rule of the world devolves upon the proletariat alone because it is the most numerous. A manifesto of the [Central Committee] read, "The Commune means the revolutionary proletariat armed with a dictatorship for the annihilation of privileges and the destruction of the middle class." Granted that the pronouncement was made before the Commune and that the formula was established a long time ago, it nevertheless became the starting point and the doctrine of the International. I find it clearly expressed in a letter that a worker in Reims wrote to [one of the founders of the International, Louis] Varlin on March 10, 1870. . . .

"We are the ones who make life possible in every nation. Without us, nothing could exist. . . . We are the *majority*, we are *power*, we represent *equity*, we are *justice*, we are the

[1] Denis Poulot, *Le sublime* (Paris, 1870), p. 180. [A long forgotten book that is now regarded as containing a better insight into social and economic conditions than did the novels of Emile Zola. Editor's note.]

universal morality, and a cause as just as ours must not succumb."
Such men are pretenders. The high opinion they have of themselves precludes labor and suits them only for the highest roles.
Their ambitions are the more extreme in that they are founded
on illusions. They believe in their future, they define it, and they
move toward it. In their own way, they are fanatics. . . .

What the Commune stood for, and continues to stand for, is
instant substitution of the proletariat for all other classes of society, in ownership, in administration, in the excercise of power.
The methods to be used to achieve its end we already know; the
programs to be instituted have already been cited. The lead is
taken by men whose career is conspiracy. They are indifferent
to the form of government they are attacking. We saw the Republic of 1848 arrest, execute, and deport conspirators who had
wanted to overturn the monarchy simply because is was a monarchy, just as the Republic of 1871 has arrested, executed, and
deported conspirators who had attacked the Empire. [But these
matters are mere pretexts, just as wars, defeats, and national
calamities only provide opportunities for the revolutionaries.]
The fundamental causation is more remote and more basic and
is within man himself. The publishers of the *Bulletin de la Commune* were right to claim that "the general origin of the communal movement of 1871 is as old as the world." In fact, it goes
back to the time of *Genesis*, dating from the day that Cain killed
his brother. Envy is behind their claims, . . . an original sin that
propels mean souls and dubious minds. This quality has no particular name, but could be called Cainism. It was responsible
for the September massacres [1792] . . . and for the Commune.
It is not limited to France, but is everywhere. . . .

They become collectivists, whether they be the Communards of France, the Social Democrats of Germany, or the Ni-
hilists of Russia. The names change, but the tendencies are the
same. We alone do not suffer from this illness, for other nations
are hardly any better off than we are. If one is to argue that our
defeats, meaning the loss of two provinces and a crushing indemnity, determined the nature of the Commune, how is it that the
acquisition of the two provinces and the exorbitant indemnity

unleashed the ferocity of the Social Democrats in Germany?[2]
. . . Not only victorious Germany but victorious Russia
[who defeated Turkey in 1877] lives under the threat of
systematic assassination and chaos. An attempt has been made
on the King in Italy too, and Spain also has her regicide. In the
aftermath of these crimes, the Communards sing hosanna and insist that their time is near. . . . If such men are mad, as
some alienists are claiming, they are dangerous madmen, fit for
strait jackets.

No doubt there were some madmen in the Communal flock.
There were also the bewildered, the unintelligent who joined
the adventure without considering where it would lead them;
the down-and-out, left to their own resources, not knowing
where their next piece of bread would come from and ready
for any insurrection to come along. Such as these are entitled to
pity, for [society] has the means to detach them from the revolutionary movement, but did nothing for them. More prominent, however, were the vain who strutted in the limelight,
smitten by their new ranks, drunk with self-importance, super-
numeraries playing majors and colonels, . . . seeing in the
great upheaval little more than the right to wear the fine boots
that delighted them. Alongside these beplumed bad actors were
the numerous men at war with the law, now free and . . .
determined to undermine a society that has courts to try thieves
and maintains prisons to lock them up. But all of these constituted an army, a reserve force ready for insurrection, the likes
of which exist in every overpopulated city. But they were not
the Commune.

By the Commune I mean a group of seven to eight hundred im-
passioned individuals, seized by ambition, actually aloof from
the people in whose name they spoke, hating the rich whom they
envied, and ready for anything in order to become famous, to
make themselves obeyed, and to become dictators. Some were

[2] Two attempts were made on the life of Emperor William I in 1878, on
May 11 by a deranged radical, Emil Hödel, and on June 27 by Dr. Karl
Nobiling, the latter wounding the Emperor seriously. Alexander II of
Russia had also survived several attempts on his life, although he would fall
victim to assassins later in 1881. (Editor's note.)

petty bourgeois on the skids, some were workers frustrated by failure to become proprietors, some were proprietors who had failed to make an anticipated great fortune; there were newspapermen without newspapers, doctors without patients, schoolmasters without pupils: Rigault, Ferré, Ranvier, Parisel, Pillot, Urbain, Gaillard, Trinquet, Eudes, Gois, Mégy, Sérizier[3], those who stood outside humanity and whose crimes will haunt them eternally. An amnesty would return them to the very country they were pledged to ruin, to the city they wished to destroy. Then universal suffrage, however unconsciously—but certainly irresponsibly—would be able to pick them up again and to make of them town councilmen, deputies, senators, presidents of committees of public safety, not that that would suffice to cleanse them. For they have such bloodstains on their hands that not all the water in the sea could wash them away, and they are so impregnated with the smell of kerosene that it will never evaporate.

Confronted by both history and morality, [the Communards] will forever be what their actions made them: traitors to their wounded country, arsonists, and murderers.

8   *Jules Claretie*

Jules Claretie (1840-1913) was a provincial (Limoges) who made a career in Parisian journalism under his own name and using several pseudonyms. Also a writer of novels and histories, he was a man of great energy and verve, pouring forth prose that is now largely forgotten. Yet it earned him election to the French Academy in 1888. The Du Camp work was published after Lissagaray's volume and at

---

[3] He names some of the more violent personalities in Paris, most of them Blanquists or Jacobins. (Editor's note.)

SOURCE. Jules Claretie, *Histoire de la Révolution de 1870–1871*, Paris: le Journal *l'Eclipse*, 1872, Vol. II, pp. 651–652. Translated for this book by Roger L. Williams. Copyright 1872 by *l'Eclipse*.

a moment when the amnesty question was a hot political issue; where-
as Claretie's anti-Communard history, from which the following
extract is taken, was published much earlier. Even so, Claretie knew
Lissagaray's point of view, thanks to a limited study of the Commune
published in Brussels in 1871.

The mob, being inordinately unstable and vulnerable to every impetus, yet itself incapable of providing any determined or lasting direction, was the victim of speakers, publicists, and newsmongers, accepting and repeating everything in good faith. Speaking before the various popular clubs, then meeting in the churches, orators from the Commune would announce the victory of the Commune in Marseille, the defection of an entire Versaillese army corps, an overwhelming victory by the National Guards, of the resignation or death of [Marshal] MacMahon. Every fantasy seemed to be plausible, every tale was converted into history. This charged-up, overheated society acclaimed and voted for every motion, declared as outlaws (indeed, more than that, as beneath humanity) those Parisian deputies guilty of remaining with the Assembly in Versailles: Louis Blanc, Schoelcher, Brisson, Quinet, etc. On another occasion, the execution of the Archbishop of Paris was voted in case Versailles should not release Citizen Blanqui within forty-eight hours.

The leading clubs met in the Saint-Nicolas Church, in the Saint-Eustache Church, as well as in the traditional popular meeting places. Newer and older clubs were organized: the Old Oak, the Black Butt, the Descendants of Marat, the Sons at Duchêne, the Good Patriots of Montmartre—this last composed exclusively of women—and the Martyrs Club situated on the third floor of a wretched house in the rue Berzélius. All these clubs were the instruments of hotheads with wild ambitions. A former gunner with the National Guard, driven from his battery for cowardice, spoke loudly of his courage. A former Bonapartist agent insisted that the hostages be put to death.

. . . One evening a speaker at Saint-Eustache explained in a rather mystical way the red flag [floating over the scene]: "The noble Thiers has dared to call the red flag a *hideous flag.* Why

hideous? Both the white flag and the tricolor have had their days
of glory. But one fell into the mud in 1830, the other in shame at
Sedan and at Metz. What kind of squeamishness is this that repu-
diates the red flag, which is the people's flag!" Then turning
toward the altar with a burst of bizarre exaltation and unusual
religiosity, he cried out, "I invoke You, Christ, You who have
shed Your blood for us. We have dyed the people's standard with
the color of Your blood. You will not betray us, for You were a
child of the people!"

On another evening, at St.-Nicolas-des-Champs, a jewellry
worker, a fine speaker if a coarse one, but one never seen on the
barricades, harangued an audience that was alarmed by his bold-
ness: "You ask me, do you, what must be done to bourgeois
traitors! Well, they must be dragged before the city hall in
each arondissement and—listen carefully—there s . . . . . . with
twelve bullets in each belly! And do you know who will
make up the execution squad? The women, citizenesses, they
must be women!" . . . But give a thought to the poor
people, on occasion swayed by such fiery orators, themselves
so skilled in avoiding the mêlées [they stir up] in which labor-
ers, workers, poor dupes shed their blood and die! And when we
think that women applauded such words, . . . and remember squads of armed women, dressed up with scarfs around their
waists and adorned with red cockades, running through the
streets not unlike hysterics in politics, preparing for the im-
placable resistance of [that] last week, we can only wonder from
what slime the human species is made and about what perverse
instincts, hidden and ineradicable, still crouch in the dark soul of
mankind!

But even more shocking than these furious harangues was the
contrast provided by the pleasures that the same insurgents found
time for amid the horrors of civil war. They had celebrations,
organized concerts. They were singing, two steps away from the
dead, all of whom were French. The Tuileries, palace of the
kings taken by popular assault, was illuminated for ceremonies,
where Citizeness Agar spoke the verses of Auguste Barbier,
where, under its gilded arches, Citizeness Bordas sang the boom-
ing refrains of la Canaille (the Riff-raff). No one could fail to
be struck by the frightful, sinister contrast: the Tuileries, now

rank with the stink of the people, its corridors formerly streaming with white shoulders and heady scents.

Strange and frightening times, well calculated to break the heart and for a moment to make us despair for virtue, for pity, for goodness, for all those things that make life peaceful and possible: a smile, solace, humanitarianism. Yet they found time to laugh, to listen to verses about fairyland, while shells were destroying Neuilly, while guns on the walls of Paris were digging holes in French breasts, while the ghastly performance played on.

Matters had come, however, to a difficult pass for the Commune. Beginning on May 7, a strong battery of seventy high-calibre guns at Montretout was hitting [Parisian fortifications]. Under this terrible fire, Paris was living silent and as if stunned by the formidable concert of explosions. Porte Maillot was riddled from [the captured] Fort Mont-Valérien. The Issy, Vanves, and Montrouge forts were hard pressed, Fort Issy hardly firing any longer. . . . And it had become impossible to supply Fort Issy. On the road between Vanves and Clamart, all convoys were being intercepted. Then, on the morning of May 9, the officers from Issy slipped away, followed by their men . . . . Shortly after, the vacated fort was entered by [Versaillese] infantry, where they found a considerable quanity of ammunition, rations, and guns and *mitrailleuses* in large number, some of the guns dismounted, their barrels smashed and bloodied.

On learning of the loss of Fort Issy, [General] Rossel was overcome with violent anger. He had been trying in vain to put together a force of 12,000 men to relieve the fort. Now he grabbed a pen and wrote this dispatch intended for public display. "The Tricolor now floats over Fort Issy." M. Vésinier tried to give the lie to this dispatch in his newspaper, to insist that Issy still belonged to the Commune, but in vain.[1] The population soon learned that Rossel had told the truth, and rumors of treason began circulating about Rossel. Vallès and Pyat both accused

---

[1] The Jacobin Pierre Vésinier, a vicious personality who was simultaneously publisher of *Paris-Libre* and the Editor-in-Chief of the Commune's *Journal officiel*, famous for character assassination. (Editor's note.)

him.[2] Rossel then wrote a letter in which he plainly asked to be put in jail. . . . Several months later, Rossel, then on the eve of death, wrote of his recollections:

"It is with real disgust that I review the swift events of that brief period, and such a sentiment perhaps prevents me from detailing those events as I should wish. The memory of all those presumptious revolutionaries, devoid of knowledge and energy, perhaps capable of a bold stroke, but incapable of resolution and firm purpose, remains a nightmare for me. I served the Revolution faithfully, even blindly, to a point where I myself experienced all of the hopes that were bound up in this endeavor. The Commune had no statesmen, had no soldiers, and wanted neither; it only destroyed, having neither the power nor even the will to create anew. This oligarchy was the most odious despotism that can be imagined, fearful of publicity because it was aware of its own folly, and an enemy of liberty because of its unstable state that made it vulnerable to any disturbance. Its procedures of government being limited to keeping the people loyal, [the Commune] bled the people of their savings, ruining their futures also by unaccustoming them to working. When I realized that the evil was without remedy, that all efforts, all sacrifices were useless, my role came to an end."

His role had, indeed, come to an end, but the actor was going to pay for it dearly. A grain of sand caught up in the popular torrent, he ultimately found himself cast aside and then ground to bits. His was a cruel destiny that ought to serve as a lesson to us all. For it reveals that a lofty soul, a strong character, even the gift of genius, come to nothing if they are not acompanied by those humbler and surer virtues that make nations great and men truly strong: the habit of patience and respect for one's duty.

[2] Jules Vallès, one of the most prominent of the Proudhonians, and Félix Pyat, a Jacobin who favored the use of terror, both of them journalists. (Editor's note.)

PART TWO

Major Early Interpretations That
Contributed to Mythologies
about the Commune

1 FROM   *Karl Marx*
The Socialist Myth

Karl Marx (1818-1883), the well-known socialist revolutionary and philosopher, was also a master of polemical writing. The address, from which this extract is drawn, was presented by him to the General Council of the First International on May 30, 1871, two days after the Commune had come to its end. Lenin would later say that the young Soviet Republic stood on the shoulders of the Paris Commune, an accurate measure of the importance of the Marxian interpretation of the Paris Commune for Soviet ideology.

On the dawn of the 18th of March, Paris arose to the thunderburst of "Vive la Commune!" What is the Commune, that sphinx so tantalising to the bourgeois mind?

"The proletarians of Paris," said the Central Comittee in its manifesto of the 18th March, "amidst the failures and treasons of the ruling classes, have understood that the hour has struck for them to save the situation by taking into their own hands the direction of public affairs. . . . They have understood that it is their imperious duty and their absolute right to render themselves masters of their own destinies, by seizing upon the governmental power." But the working class cannot simply lay hold of the ready-made state machinery, and wield it for its own purposes.

The centralised state power, with its ubiquitous organs of standing army, police, bureaucracy, clergy, and judicature—organs wrought after the plan of a systematic and hierarchic division of labour—orginates from the days of absolute monarchy, serving nascent middle class society as a mighty weapon in its struggles against feudalism. Still, its development remained clogged by all manner of mediæval rubbish, seignorial rights, local

SOURCE. Karl Marx, *The Civil War in France*, New York: International Publishers, 1940, pp. 54–69. Reprinted by permission of International Publishers Co., Inc. Copyright © 1940 by International Publishers, Inc. Third printing, 1962.

privileges, municipal and guild monopolies and provincial con-
stitutions. The gigantic broom of the French Revolution of the
eighteenth century swept away all these relics of bygone times,
thus clearing simultaneously the social soil of its last hindrances
to the superstructure of the modern state edifice raised under the
First Empire, itself the offspring of the coalition wars of old
semi-feudal Europe against modern France. During the subsequent *régimes* the government, placed under parliamentary control—that is, under the direct control of the propertied classes—
became not only a hotbed of huge national debts and crushing
taxes; with its irresistible allurements of place, pelf, and patronage, it became not only the bone of contention between the rival
factions and adventurers of the ruling classes; but its political
character changed simultaneously with the economic changes
of society. At the same pace at which the progress of modern
industry developed, widened, intensified the class antagonism
between capital and labour, the state power assumed more
and more the character of the national power of capital over
labour, of a public force organised for social enslavement, of
an engine of class despotism. After every revolution marking
a progressive phase in the class struggle, the purely repressive
character of the state power stands out in bolder and bolder re-
lief. The Revolution of 1830, resulting in the transfer of government from the landlords to the capitalists, transferred it from the
more remote to the more direct antagonists of the working men.
The bourgeois republicans, who, in the name of the Revolution
of February, took the state power, used it for the June massacres, in order to convince the working class that "social" republic
meant the republic ensuring their social subjection, and in order
to convince the royalist bulk of the bourgeois and landlord class
that they might safely leave the cares and emoluments of government to the bourgeois "republicans." However, after their one
heroic exploit of June, the bourgeois republicans had, from the
front, to fall back to the rear of the "Party of Order"—a combi-
nation formed by all the rival fractions and factions of the appropriating class in their now openly declared antagonism to the
producing classes. The proper form of their joint-stock government was the *parliamentary republic*, with Louis Bonaparte for
its president. Theirs was a *régime* of avowed class terrorism and

deliberate insult towards the "vile multitude." If the parliamentary republic, as M. Thiers said, "divided them [the different fractions of the ruling class] least," it opened an abyss between that class and the whole body of society outside their spare ranks. The restraints by which their own divisions had under former *régimes* still checked the state power, were removed by their union; and in view of the threatening upheaval of the proletariat, they now used that state power mercilessly and ostentatiously as the national war engine of capital against labour. In their uninterrupted crusade against the producing masses they were, however, bound not only to invest the executive with continually increased powers of repression, but at the same time to divest their own parliamentary stronghold—the National Assembly—one by one, of all its own means of defence against the Executive. The Executive, in the person of Louis Bonaparte, turned them out. The natural offspring of the "Party of Order" republic was the Second Empire.

The empire, with the *coup d'état* for its certificate of birth, universal suffrage for its sanction, and the sword for its sceptre, professed to rest upon the peasantry, the large mass of producers not directly involved in the struggle of capital and labour. It professed to save the working class by breaking down parliamentarism, and, with it, the undisguised subserviency of government to the propertied classes. It professed to save the propertied classes by upholding their economic supremacy over the working class; and, finally, it professed to unite all classes by reviving for all the chimera of national glory. In reality, it was the only form of government possible at a time when the bourgeoisie had already lost, and the working class had not yet acquired, the faculty of ruling the nation. It was acclaimed throughout the world as the saviour of society. Under its sway, bourgeois society, freed from political cares, attained a development unexpected even by itself. Its industry and commerce expanded to colossal dimensions; financial swindling celebrated cosmopolitan orgies; the misery of the masses was set off by a shameless display of gorgeous, meretricious and debased luxury. The state power, apparently soaring high above society, was at the same time itself the greatest scandal of that society and the very hotbed of all its corruptions. Its own rottenness, and the rottenness of the society it had saved, were laid bare by the bayonet of Prussia, herself eagerly bent upon transferring the supreme seat of that *régime* from Paris to Berlin. Imperialism is, at the same time, the most prostitute and the ultimate form of the state power which nascent middle class society had commenced to elaborate as a means of its own emancipation from feudalism, and which full-grown bourgeois society had finally transformed into a means for the enslavement of labour by capital.

The direct antithesis to the empire was the Commune. The cry of "social republic" with which the Revolution of February was ushered in by the Paris proletariat, did but express a vague aspiration after a republic that was not only to supersede the monarchical form of class rule, but class rule itself. The Commune was the positive form of that republic.

Paris, the central seat of the old governmental power, and, at the same time, the social stronghold of the French working class, had risen in arms against the attempt of Thiers and the Rurals to restore and perpetuate that old governmental power bequeathed to them by the empire. Paris could resist only because, in consequence of the siege, it had got rid of the army, and replaced it by a National Guard, the bulk of which consisted of working men. This fact was now to be transformed into an institution. The first decree of the Commune, therefore, was the suppression of the standing army, and the substitution for it of the armed people.

The Commune was formed of the municipal councillors, chosen by universal suffrage in the various wards of the town, responsible and revocable at short terms. The majority of its members were naturally working men, or acknowledged representatives of the working class. The Commune was to be a working, not a parliamentary body, executive and legislative at the same time. Instead of continuing to be the agent of the Central Government, the police was at once stripped of its political attributes, and turned into the responsible and at all times revocable agent of the Commune. So were the officials of all other branches of the administration. From the members of the Commune downwards, the public service had to be done at *workmen's wages*. The vested interests and the representation allowances of the high dignitaries of state disappeared along with the high dignitaries themselves. Public functions ceased to be the private property of the tools of the

Central Government. Not only municipal administration, but the whole initiative hitherto exercised by the state was laid into the hands of the Commune.

Having once got rid of the standing army and the police, the physical force elements of the old government, the Commune was anxious to break the spiritual force of repression, the "parson-power," by the disestablishment and disendowment of all churches as proprietary bodies. The priests were sent back to the recesses of private life, there to feed upon the alms of the faithful in imitation of their predecessors, the apostles. The whole of the educational institutions were opened to the people gratuitously, and at the same time cleared of all interference of church and state. Thus, not only was education made accessible to all, but science itself freed from the fetters which class prejudice and governmental force had imposed upon it.

The judicial functionaries were to be divested of that sham independence which had but served to mask their abject subserviency to all succeeding governments to which, in turn, they had taken, and broken, the oaths of allegiance. Like the rest of public servants, magistrates and judges were to be elective, responsible and revocable.

The Paris Commune was, of course, to serve as a model to all the great industrial centres of France. The communal régime once established in Paris and the secondary centres, the old centralised government would in the provinces, too, have to give way to the self-government of the producers. In a rough sketch of national organisation which the Commune had no time to develop, it states clearly that the Commune was to be the political form of even the smallest country hamlet, and that in the rural districts the standing army was to be replaced by a national militia, with an extremely short term of service. The rural communes of every district were to administer their common affairs by an assembly of delegates in the central town, and these district assemblies were again to send deputies to the National Delegation in Paris, each delegate to be at any time revocable and bound by the mandat imperatif (formal instructions) of his constituents. The few but important functions which still would remain for a central government were not to be suppressed, as has been intentionally misstated, but were to be discharged by Communal and therefore strictly responsible agents. The unity of the nation was not to be broken, but, on the contrary, to be organised by the Communal Constitution, and to become a reality by the destruction of the state power which claimed to be the embodiment of that unity independent of, and superior to, the nation itself, from which it was but a parasitic excrescence. While the merely repressive organs of the old governmental power were to be amputated, its legitimate functions were to be wrested from an authority usurping pre-eminence over itself, and restored to the responsible agents of society. Instead of deciding once in three or six years which member of the ruling class was to misrepresent the people in Parliament, universal suffrage was to serve the people, constituted in Communes, as individual suffrage serves every other employer in the search for the workmen and managers in his business. And it is well known that companies, like individuals, in matters of real business generally know how to put the right man in the right place, and, if they for once make a mistake, to redress it promptly. On the other hand, nothing could be more foreign to the spirit of the Commune than to supersede universal suffrage by hierarchic investiture. . . .

The multiplicity of interpretations to which the Commune has been subjected, and the multiplicity of interests which construed it in their favour, show that it was a thoroughly expansive political form, while all previous forms of government had been emphatically repressive. Its true secret was this. It was essentially a working class government, the produce of the struggle of the producing against the appropriating class, the political form at last discovered under which to work out the economical emancipation of labour.

Except on this last condition, the Communal Constitution would have been an impossibility and a delusion. The political rule of the producer cannot co-exist with the perpetuation of his social slavery. The Commune was therefore to serve as a lever for uprooting the economical foundations upon which rests the existence of classes, and therefore of class rule. With labour emancipated, every man becomes a working man, and productive labour ceases to be a class attribute.

It is a strange fact. In spite of all the tall talk and all the immense literature, for the last sixty years, about emancipation of labour, no sooner do the working men anywhere take the subject into their own hands with a will, than uprises at once all the apologetic phraseology of the mouthpieces of present society with its two poles of capital and wage-slavery (the landlord now is but the sleeping partner of the capitalist), as if capitalist society was still in its purest state of virgin innocence, with its antagonisms still undeveloped, with its delusions still unexploded, with its prostitute realities not yet laid bare. The Commune, they exclaim, intends to abolish property, the basis of all civilisation! Yes, gentlemen, the Commune intended to abolish that class property which makes the labour of the many the wealth of the few. It aimed at the expropriation of the expropriators. It wanted to make individual property a truth by transforming the means of production, land and capital, now chiefly the means of enslaving and exploiting labour, into mere instruments of free and associated labour. But this is communism, "impossible" communism! Why, those members of the ruling classes who are intelligent enough to perceive the impossibility of continuing the present system—and they are many—have become the obtrusive and full-mouthed apostles of co-operative production. If co-operative production is not to remain a sham and a snare; if it is to supersede the capitalist system; if united co-operative societies are to regulate national production upon a common plan, thus taking it under their own control, and putting an end to the constant anarchy and periodical convulsions which are the fatality of capitalist production—what else, gentlemen, would it be but communism, "possible" communism?

The working class did not expect miracles from the Commune. They have no ready-made utopias to introduce *par decret du peuple*. They know that in order to work out their own emancipation, and along with it that higher form to which present society is irresistibly tending by its own economical agencies, they will have to pass through long struggles, through a series of historic processes, transforming circumstances and men. They have no ideals to realise, but to set free the elements of the new society with which old collapsing bourgeois society itself is pregnant. In the full consciousness of their historic mission, and with the heroic resolve to act up to it, the working class can afford to smile at the coarse invective of the gentlemen's gentlemen with the pen and inkhorn, and at the didactic patronage of well-wishing bourgeois-doctrinaires, pouring forth their ignorant platitudes and sectarian crotchets in the oracular tone of scientific infallibility.

When the Paris Commune took the management of the revolution in its own hands; when plain working men for the first time dared to infringe upon the governmental privilege of their "natural superiors," and, under circumstances of unexampled difficulty, performed their work modestly, conscientiously, and efficiently—performed it at salaries the highest of which barely amounted to one-fifth of what, according to high scientific authority, is the minimum required for a secretary to a certain metropolitan school-board—the old world writhed in convulsions of rage at the sight of the Red Flag, the symbol of the Republic of Labour, floating over the Hôtel de Ville. . . .

If the Commune was thus the true representative of all the healthy elements of French society, and therefore the truly national government, it was, at the same time, as a working men's government, as the bold champion of the emancipation of labour, emphatically international. Within sight of the Prussian army, that had annexed to Germany two French provinces, the Commune annexed to France the working people all over the world.

The Second Empire had been the jubilee of cosmopolitan blackleggism, the rakes of all countries rushing in at its call for a share in its orgies and in the plunder of the French people. Even at this moment the right hand of Thiers is Ganessco, the foul Wallachian, and his left hand is Markovsky, the Russian spy. The Commune admitted all foreigners to the honour of dying for an immortal cause. Between the foreign war lost by their treason, and the civil war fomented by their conspiracy with the foreign invader, the bourgeoisie had found the time to display their patriotism by organising police hunts upon the Germans in France. The Commune made a German working man its Minister of Labour. Thiers, the bourgeoisie, the Second Empire, had continually deluded Poland by loud professions of sympathy, while in reality betraying her to, and doing the dirty work of, Russia. The Commune honoured the heroic sons of Poland by placing them at the head of the defenders of Paris. And, to broadly mark the new era of history it was conscious of initiating, under the eyes of the conquering Prussians on the one side, and of the Bonapartist army, led by Bonapartist generals, on the other, the Commune pulled down that colossal symbol of martial glory, the Vendôme Column. The great social measure of the Commune was its own working existence. Its special measures could but betoken the tendency of a government of the people by the people. Such were the abolition of the nightwork of journeymen bakers; the prohibition, under penalty, of the employers' practice to reduce wages by levying upon their workpeople fines under manifold pretexts—a process in which the employer combines in his own person the parts of legislator, judge, and executor, and filches the money to boot. Another measure of this class was the surrender to associations of workmen, under reserve of compensation, of all closed workshops and factories, no matter whether the respective capitalists had absconded or preferred to strike work.

The financial measures of the Commune, remarkable for their sagacity and moderation, could only be such as were compatible with the state of a besieged town. Considering the colossal robberies committed upon the city of Paris by the great financial companies and contractors, under the protection of Haussmann, the Commune would have had an incomparably better title to confiscate their property than Louis Napoleon had against the Orleans family. . . .[1]

In every revolution there intrude, at the side of its true agents, men of a different stamp; some of them survivors of and devotees to past revolutions, without insight into the present movement, but preserving popular influence by their known honesty and courage, or by the sheer force of tradition; others mere brawlers, who, by dint of repeating year after year the same set of stereotyped declamations against the government of the day, have sneaked into the reputation of revolutionists of the first water. After the 18th of March, some such men did also turn up, and in some cases contrived to play pre-eminent parts. As far as their power went, they hampered the real action of the working class, exactly as men of that sort have hampered the full development

[1] Baron Georges Haussmann was the rebuilder of Paris during the Second Empire. Marx also refers here to a controversial decision to confiscate Orleans property in 1852. (Editor's note.)

of every previous revolution. They are an unavoidable evil: with time they are shaken off; but time was not allowed to the Commune.

Wonderful, indeed, was the change the Commune had wrought in Paris! No longer any trace of the meretricious Paris of the Second Empire! No longer was Paris the rendezvous of British landlords, Irish absentees, American ex-slaveholders and shoddy men, Russian ex-serfowners, and Wallachian boyards. No more corpses at the morgue, no nocturnal burglaries, scarcely any robberies; in fact, for the first time since the days of February 1848, the streets of Paris were safe, and that without any police of any kind. "We," said a member of the Commune, "hear no longer of assassination, theft and personal assault; it seems indeed as if the police had dragged along with it to Versailles all its Conservative friends." The *cocottes* had refound the scent of their protectors—the absconding men of family, religion, and, above all, of property. In their stead, the real women of Paris showed again at the surface—heroic, noble, and devoted, like the women of antiquity. Working, thinking, fighting, bleeding Paris—almost forgetful, in its incubation of a new society, of the cannibals at its gates—radiant in the enthusiasm of its historic initiative!

Opposed to this new world at Paris, behold the old world at Versailles—that assembly of the ghouls of all defunct *régimes,* Legitimists and Orleanists, eager to feed upon the carcass of the nation—with a tail of antediluvian republicans, sanctioning, by their presence in the Assembly, the slaveholders' rebellion, relying for the maintenance of their parliamentary republic upon the vanity of the senile mountebank at its head, and caricaturing 1789 by holding their ghastly meetings in the *Jeu de Paume.*[2] There it was, this Assembly, the representative of everything dead in France, propped up to the semblance of life by nothing but the swords of the generals of Louis Bonaparte. Paris all truth, Versailles all lie; and that lie vented through the mouth of Thiers.

Thiers tells a deputation of the mayors of the Seine-et-Oise— "You may rely upon my word, which I have *never* broken!" He

---

[2] The royal tennis court at Versailles where the National Assembly had convened in 1789. (Editor's note.)

tells the Assembly itself that "it was the most freely elected and most liberal Assembly France ever possessed"; he tells his motley soldiery that it was "the admiration of the world, and the finest army France ever possessed"; he tells the provinces that the bombardment of Paris by him was a myth: "If some cannon-shots have been fired, it is not the deed of the army of Versailles, but of some insurgents trying to make believe that they are fighting, while they dare not show their faces." He again tells the provinces that "the artillery of Versailles does not bombard Paris, but only cannonades it." He tells the Archbishop of Paris that the pretended executions and reprisals (!) attributed to the Versailles troops were all moonshine. He tells Paris that he was only anxious "to free it from the hideous tyrants who oppress it," and that, in fact, the Paris of the Commune was "but a handful of criminals."

The Paris of M. Thiers was not the real Paris of the "vile multitude," but a phantom Paris, the Paris of the *francs-fileurs*, the Paris of the Boulevards, male and female—the rich, the capitalist, the gilded, the idle Paris, now thronging with its lackeys, its blacklegs, its literary *bôhème*, and its *cocottes* at Versailles, Saint-Denis, Rueil, and Saint-Germain; considering the civil war but an agreeable diversion, eyeing the battle going on through telescopes, counting the rounds of cannon, and swearing by their own honour and that of their prostitutes, that the performance was far better got up than it used to be at the Porte St. Martin.[3] The men who fell were really dead; the cries of the wounded were cries in good earnest; and, besides, the whole thing was so intensely historical.

3 A well-known theater. (Editor's note.)

2 FROM   *The Daru Report*
                 The Reactionary Myth

*The Daru Committee, which submitted its report to the National
Assembly on December 22, 1871, was created by the Assembly on
June 17, 1871, and charged to inquire at length into the origins of what
was then officially called the Insurrection of March 18. Its chairman,
Comte Napoleon Daru (1807-1890), had been a member of the Cham-
ber of Peers from 1832 to 1848. Elected to represent La Manche in
the National Assembly in 1848 and again in 1849, he went into retire-
ment after the coup d'état of 1851 to do historical writing, which won
him election to the* Académie des sciences morales et politiques *in
1860. He returned to politics as a liberal opponent of the Empire in
1869 and became a member of the Ollivier cabinet in 1870. Elected
to the National Assembly in 1871, he was known as an Orleanist, a
man whose views were similar to those of Adolphe Thiers. The following extract, from Chapter Nine of the report, shows the essential
conservatism of the old liberal position.*

We are faced with a new invasion by barbarians. They are not
at our doors, but amongst us—in our villages, in our homes.
Unlike their predecessors of the fourth and fifth centuries, they
do not come to bring regenerating blood to an aged world. They
come with fire and sword. They do not so much wish to destroy
the city of stone as the city of morality. Denying those truths
that have to date been the honor of the human race, they attack
the principles of property and family, the secular bases of every
society, and do not believe in the existence of God or in the
immortality of the soul. Seeing no distinction between good and
evil, denying the possibility of freedom or moral consideration
in human actions, they expose to the full light of day the corrup-

SOURCE. The Daru Committee, *Enquête parlementaire sur l'insurrection
du 18 mars*, Versailles: Cerf, 1872, Vol. I, pp. 187–191 and 218–227. Translated for this book by Roger L. Williams.

tion, the meanness, the savage instincts that hitherto have remained inadmissible even in the lowest ranks of society.

The Commune of Paris has just shown [us] insane theories at work, false programs whose realization would set humanity back several centuries. It cannot too often be repeated to these alchemists of progress that the ideas, in the name of which the insurrection of March 18 was justified, are hardly new. The world has known them from its beginning, and they have come to the surface in the midst of every great crisis humanity has experienced, in the Orient as in the West, in ancient and in modern times. They can be found in the Egypt of the third and fourth centuries when the philosophical schools of Alexandria were flourishing. The Middle Ages, Germany of the sixteenth century, and England in the eighteenth century have had their socialists, who thought and behaved like those in our time. Volumes have been written on all the problems called social. Utopians in every epoch, philosophers and thinkers in every country, have been concerned for them. What is new is not contemporary socialism, but the truly formidable and organized army put at its service by the International. The danger lies not in the ideas of the sect but in the opportunities that modern science offers the members of the International to enhance their meetings and their propaganda. Thanks to the unity of French society, to widespread coverage by the press, and to the ease of communication in every form, the socialist appeal resounds continually everywhere, so that the very triumphs of civilization are used against it. Railroads, electricity, and steam power become the means in the attempt to return us to barbarism. The enemies of society today can organize international conspiracies and increase their attacks with such swiftness that the forces of resistance find themselves paralyzed at those points where it pleases [the enemy] to direct his blows unexpectedly. The danger thus lies in an instrument put at the disposition of the unenlightened masses, at the disposition of those whom M. Thiers twenty years ago called *the vile multitude*,[1] *the vile populace*,[2] those who, despite the progress

[1] In a parliamentary debate over the Law of May 31, 1850, to restrict the suffrage. (Editor's note.)

[2] In Thiers' *Histoire de la Révolution* (1823–1827), in his account of the death of Louis XVI. (Editor's note.)

of knowledge, are as easy to mislead and to win over today as ever before. This instrument is universal suffrage. As soon as the absolute sovereignty of numbers is proclaimed, it suffices to spread a false idea quickly and extensively enough to have it pass as fact before the minority can begin to protest and before the majority can come to realize that it has been mistaken; especially, if you put a gun and the vote in the same hand, that is, the temptation and the possibility of making that idea prevail with the aid of force.

In confusing the true with the false, the socialists find support in one of man's instincts: his love for his fellow creatures. They can attract the masses by promising to erase all inequalities, to remove all of those ills that hinder the human race. Is this noble ambition obtainable? Can the faith in unending progress sustain [the radicals] in the face of the spectacle to which we have been the appalled witnesses? In any case, and despite what progress has been made, it is quite impossible to forget that evil dispositions are still with us, in all their primitive energy, when we see some of the learned, some of the civilized, commit the atrocities of May, 1871.

The various schools of socialism are based on a doctrine that can be summed up in a few words: all men have a right to happiness, an equal and absolute right. Happiness means the enjoyment of all of the natural or primitive goods as well as those created by man's labor, an enjoyment limited only by individual needs and desires. Since man's existence is limited to this life, there being no future, there can be no compensation awaiting anyone frustrated in his share of [earthly] enjoyment. Thus, it is necessary that society be organized in such a way that nothing can be an obstacle to the desires of any of its members. By dint of accumulated work over several successive generations, these goods have become the property of certain men, of certain families, or of certain classes. For the socialists, this ownership violates the primordial right of all men of the same generation to enjoy equally the common treasure of mankind. It logically follows that property must be abolished as the obstacle to [this] right; and that everyone, in being born, acquires the right to take his proportional share of the goods accumulated by the labor of previous generations. Thus, every socialist system, what-

ever the means it extols, arrives at the same end: the abolition of
all personal and hereditary property, as well as all social institutions that are based upon property.

These great promoters of progress thus begin by denying that
which has been mankind's strength and greatness: the possibility
for each generation to survive itself and to continue on in some
manner by creating the intellectual or material means that will
contribute both to the progress and to the happiness of the coming generation. That is what makes the family and the state—for
the state is only the government of a larger family—makes property, heredity, the fatherland, history, and all those traditions of
the mind and spirit that constitute the continuous life of a people
despite the rapid extinction of generations. The cultists of our
day abolish all of these things, no longer merely in theory or in
philosophical books, but in practice and in reality.

The only reason for the International to exist is to lend strength
to these sorry doctrines and to provide the greatest possible
means to see to it that this covetousness, which they call rights,
shall prevail. It is in vain that the founders [of the International]
described it as a study group.[3] If, and we recognize it happily,
there were among them those who sought in good faith and
with laudable means the improvement of the workers' lot, they
had to give way before an increasing insistence on the primacy
of force and sheer numbers as the right way to secure the sharing
of the goods of this world. It is no less true that the International
created means of propaganda to serve socialism all out of proportion to what we have hitherto known. It feigned to act only
in the name of justice and truth, yet stirred up the most brutal
passions! It spoke in the name of rights, yet in reality was only
concerned to serve [certain] interests. The questions that [the
International] raises and the solutions that it advances would be
too horrifying if its doctors were to present them naked. Thus
they are concealed in formulas borrowed from the science of
economics! It is equally incontestable that at the bottom of all
the International's programs is the cult of materialism, the nega-
tion of all faith, the destruction of capital and of inheritance.

---

[3] Seeking to comply with the restrictive labor laws of the Second Empire,
the earliest French adherents to the International did seek to be recognized
simply as study groups. (Editor's note.)

Self-interest, greatly excited, blinds and misleads the masses. The desire to share effortlessly in all the goods accumulated by prior work is patently absurd, whether from the practical or the theoretical point of view. But the alchemists of the new sect are not bothered by that, for they only see the ends to which they aspire: the immediate and instant improvement of their lot. . . .

Toward the end of the Second Empire, the International had made such progress that its leaders believed that they had achieved sufficient support to make their ideas prevail. They had created a state within the State. They knew it and said so, and were confident of substituting their organization and power for those of the official state. Nothing equals the suspicion that they showed for the policies of the Left, for those who then called themselves the Irreconcilables.[4] The social revolution would be easily accomplished, they thought, through the unanimous co-operation of the proletarians. They hoped to avoid a struggle, but if it had to come, they would hold the possessing classes responsible for it for failure to surrender upon demand. "We understand the red flag to be the symbol of universal love," stated one of the International's publications. "Let our enemies take care not to transform it into a flag of terror for themselves!" They began the war against the bourgeoisie . . . in their writing, waiting until they could begin it with force.

On January 8, 1869, on the eve of the [national] elections, [the Proudhonian] E.-L. Varlin wrote, "We shall enter the electoral contest with the bourgeois Republicans of all shades in order to make clearer the schism between the people and the bourgeoisie." . . . [And Gustave] Cluseret [a member of the International since 1867] wrote a letter to Varlin on February 17 [1870] . . . that proves that the crimes of the Commune of Paris were premeditated. Foreseeing that the time was near when the members of the International would commence action, the self-styled general[5] wrote: "On that day we must be both physically and mentally ready. On that day, it will be all or nothing!

---

[4] The Moderate Republican opponents of the Second Empire, who were often opposed by socialist candidates in the election of 1869. (Editor's note.)

[5] Cluseret briefly commanded the defense of Paris for the Commune and called himself a general. He had been an army officer, but was certainly inexperienced for command. (Editor's note.)

. . . But let me tell you, on that day Paris will either be ours or Paris will no longer exist!" . . .

During the first siege of Paris, the members of the International took little part in the revolutionary demonstrations or in the attempts upon the government. They had evidently received instructions to that effect [from the General Council of the International in London] as this letter from their French correspondent, Dupont, to Albert Richard in Lyon reveals: "The pitiful end to the imperial Soulouque,"[6] he wrote on September 7, "brings the Favres and the Gambettas to power. Nothing is changed, as the power remains in bourgeois hands. Under these circumstances, the workers' role, or rather their duty, is to allow this bourgeois vermin to make peace with the Prussians." The Socialists generally took no part in the October 31 and January 22 [insurrections], the Jacobin party alone furnishing the actors on those two days.

It appears from the minutes of the Federal Council of the International Association of Workingmen . . . that the participation of the International in the Insurrection of March 18 was considerably less, and certainly less direct, than has been generally presumed. The Parisian sections of the International appear to have been quite completely disorganized during the siege. "Since the fourth of September," [Leo] Frankel noted, "the International has ceased to function. The [Parisian] sections must be reconstituted quickly if they are to have the strength that is necessary."[7] In fact, after September 4, all the workers were enrolled in the National Guard. . . . They were preoccupied with service on the ramparts or within the city. The battalion became for them a new focus of activity, offering the possibility of exercising an immediate impact on events. It is easy to understand that they forgot about their sections. . . . Moreover, in their bivouacs, in their clubs, and in public meetings, endless social questions were the order of the day, and they had no need of further meetings to air their ideas.

Dating from the first two weeks in January, at a time when everyone realized that the siege was going to end, the leaders of

[6] Soulouque had been Emperor of Haiti. The radical opposition in France often referred to Napoleon III by that name. (Editor's note.)

[7] Minutes of February 15, 1871. (Editor's note.)

the Parisian International were busy reconstituting their association by reorganizing the sections and by finding publications to
expound their ideas and interests. They believed that they had
found their special niche in a newspaper founded by the School
of Medicine Club, named *The War to the Knife*, then enjoying
some success. [The journalist] Armand Lévy, one of the most
zealous of the Parisians in the International, offered his services
without charge, promising to fight "the clergy and their en-
croachments," and to defend the Republic "which is above
majority rights." . . . During the January 19 session, Frankel
presented the draft of a manifesto designed to announce to the
bourgeoisie the liquidation of society. Armand Lévy did not find
the wording cosmopolitan enough. According to him, "the arm
of the International ought to be extended to include the proletariat of the entire universe." . . .

On February 22, a peaceful demonstration was proposed for
the twenty-fourth designed to assert the Republicanism of the
Parisians, a demonstration that, in fact, took place. . . . And what
shows that the leaders of the Paris International were far from
believing themselves to be near the revolution of March 18 is
that one of the more important among them, Frankel, was
opposed to the proposition, urging that they ought first to
devote themselves to examining more deeply such social problems
as work stoppage and rents and that they ought to prepare a
résumé of the ideas of the International for the use of [Benoît]
Malon and [Henri-Louis] Tolain, "both sitting in the National
Assembly and who must make the will of the workers heard
there." But the Federal Council voted for the demonstration. . . .

At the March 1 session of the Federal Council, Varlin made a
proposal in the name of the Central Committee of the National
Guard, which had just been reconstituted. This was the first sign
of cooperation between the two bodies that contributed . . . to
the Insurrection of March 18. "It is urgent," Varlin began, "that
members of the International get themselves nominated within
their various companies [of the National Guards] so that they
may sit on the Central Committee." Furthermore, he asked that
four members of the International be designated a committee to
call on the Central Committee in order to find out how best the
[two bodies can be associated]. Frankel opposed the proposition,

seeing it as a compromise with the bourgeoisie, while, on the other hand, some members saw in this the opportunity to prevent the National Guard from being taken in tow by reactionaries. "Socialists," they said, "have taken the lead in this matter, and we ought to go to their aid." . . . The Federal Council then [passed the following resolution]: "A committee of four members is to be sent to the Central Committee of the National Guard, but its action will be separate and expressly limited to matters of concern to the International Association of Workingmen."

Thus, on March 1, the International seemed to pledge itself only timidly to the Central Committee and to be afraid of compromising itself in any activity that it could not exclusively control or whose goal was not entirely clear. The minutes of the March 15 session offer further proof that by that date the members of the International had no more expectation of being in control [of Paris] on the eighteenth than the leaders of the revolutionary movement did. Indeed, on March 15, after a communication from Citizens Gambon and Félix Pyat on the matter of the attitude of the National Assembly in Bordeaux, the Federal Council moved that "Pyat, Gambon, Malon, Tolain, Millière, Ranc, Tridon, Rochefort, and Langlois[8] be invited to present themselves on Wednesday, the twenty-fifth, to discuss what line should be taken." . . .

By March 22, the insurrection had succeeded, but the socialists were still not yet fully confident of their victory. During the session of the Federal Council that day, "Malon expressed the most serious doubts about the outcome of negotiations between the Arrondissement mayors and the Central Committee, and thus about the outcome of the elections to the Commune. He feared that a bloody conflict could not be avoided." The following day, Frankel proposed a manifesto urging all members of the International to vote for the Commune. His motion passed with only one dissenting vote. Another member present at the session said that he was astonished not to find a closer tie between the International and the Central Committee. "But," he added "the revolution of March 18 is entirely social, and newspapers all over

---

[8] All Parisian deputies to the National Assembly. (Editor's note.)

France are saying that the International has taken power. We know how different things are." He hoped that the Central Committee would be invited to adhere to the International, obvious proof that the two organizations were still separated, and that it was the Central Committee that had taken the initiative in the revolution. It is well known that the International succeeded in getting seventeen of its members elected to the Commune where they represented the party of social reform and were in opposition to the Majority who were the Jacobins. [We also know] that the more violent party [the Jacobins] prevailed in the Commune, but we do not precisely know to what extent the International incurred responsibility for the massacres and the fires in the midst of which the Commune perished without carrying out any of its promises to the workers. We do, however, have the sorry duty to state that [the International] has since claimed this dreadful responsibility.

PART THREE

*Recent Histories That Reflect Current
Interpretations of the Commune*

1 FROM

Frank Jellinek
Leftist View of the 1930's

Frank Jellinek (1908-   ) is a professional translator, writer and reviewer, of English origin but now residing in France. Between 1948 and 1964 he was a translator for the United Nations Secretariat. His best-known books were published in the 1930's and reflect the political climate of the Left in that era. The following extract comes from such a work, which has recently been republished as a classic from that era. Mr. Jellinek has indicated that he would somewhat alter the following pages if he now had the opportunity to rewrite them. "I do not think they are grossly inaccurate," he writes, "but I should today redistribute the emphasis in the light of all the work done on the subject since first publication in 1937." We do not, however, ask that classics be brought up to date, for it compromises their integrity.

The Commune passed in flame and fury over the scene of European politics, and vanished. Save for a small outbreak in Algeria, the Paris rising had no imitators. Only the immediate following of Karl Marx in the International even perceived the vast historical importance of the fact that the Paris workers had "stormed the heavens," as Marx put it, and for two months imposed the dictatorship of the proletariat upon the cultural capital of the world.

The immediate effect abroad of the Commune was to sharpen class antagonisms, or, at the least, to act as a touchstone for class loyalties. Workers and Liberals united in deploring the atrocities committed by both sides; but, in justice to the British bourgeois Press, it must be recorded that the surprisingly fair reports of their Paris correspondents describing the brutalities and the nau-

SOURCE. Frank Jellinek, *The Paris Commune of 1871*, London: Victor Gollancz, 1937; New York: Oxford University Press, 1937, reprinted in part, with new introduction and bibliographical notes; New York: Universal Library, Grosset & Dunlap, 1965, pp. 411–419. Reprinted by permission of Frank Jellinek. Copyright 1965 by Frank Jellinek.

seating triumph of the Versaillese did much to dampen any foreign enthusiasm for the restoration of order. The general attitude was represented by *The Times*, which published full accounts of the Versaillese jail horrors and thanked Heaven in its editorial columns that such things do not happen in England.

Punch naturally took the gentlemanly point of view. After punning in the "Assi-nine" Government[1] and the "National [Black]-guards," it depicted a righteous and rather overwhelming Britannia addressing a shrinking Republican mechanic, while she points over his head to a scene of pillage: "Is *that* the sort of thing you want, you little idiot?" Most Englishmen thought the Commune meant that the French, driven to desperation by the war, had quite simply gone mad. Earl Russell attributed the Commune to "shocking atheism."

The only organised middle-class body in England which did come out in favour of the Communards was the old Positivist Society, of which Dr. Richard Congreve, Dr. Bridges, Professor Beesly (chairman of the first meeting of the International in 1864) and Frederick Harrison were the most prominent members. Fox Bourne, who was a frequent visitor at Maitland Park and met Communard exiles with Marx there, defended the Commune in his *Examiner*. John Morley, in the *Fortnightly*, like Frederick Harrison and Whalley in the House of Commons, spoke up in favour of the social ideals which "had animated those misguided men." Beesly received from Marx thanks for his favourable articles in the *Beehive*, but also a warning that the remarkable little review was "the organ of the renegades sold out to Sam Morley," the Liberal Bristol M.P. Bradlaugh and the National Secular Society, faithful to Manchester economics, deprecated Red Republicans despite personal sympathies for some of the Communard leaders.

The International, of course, claimed the Commune as its own. As Marx declared in his *Address* of May 30: "It is but natural that members of our Association should stand in the foreground . . . wherever . . . the class struggle obtains any consistency." William Morris, Hyndman and Belfort Bax supported Marx; and Bax

---

[1] Briefly, after March 18, a metallurgical worker named Assi presided over the Central Committee of the National Guard. (Editor's note.)

boasted, apparently without any foundation, that he had converted the General Council to this view.

On the other hand, Marx perfectly correctly repudiated the common statement that the International had done anything to foster the Paris revolt. When Jules Favre, deliberately or not, confusing the International with Bakunin's Social-Democratic Alliance, expelled from the Association in 1868, sent a circular to the European Cabinets, on June 6, to invite them to destroy the International, Marx published a refutation in several London papers, including *The Times*, which drew upon that respectable organ a severe reprimand from Bob Lowe. Thiers, however, continued to let his tame propagandists foster the legend of a great "Red international conspiracy"; and the London *Observer*, in close touch with Gladstone's Government, actually threatened Marx with prosecution. For some time, Marx was, as he wrote to Kugelmann, "the best calumniated and most menaced man of London" and "a reporters' curiosity into the bargain." No prosecution, however, was attempted.

Marx's *Address* stirred up trouble within the Association. Reformists like the Republican George Odger had no stomach for a glorification of French violence, and resigned. The International replied by expelling Tolain, who had remained at Versailles to attempt conciliation. It admitted Communards besides its own members: the names of Arnaud, Cournet, Johannard, Dupont, Longuet, Ranvier, Vaillant, Franckel, LeMoussu and Serrailler are appended to the first published edition of the *Address on the Civil War in France.*

The split was largely instrumental in breaking up the First International. The Bakuninist anarchists saw in the Commune "above all, the denial of the State," and therefore disapproved of Marx's interpretation. The Italian, Spanish, Swiss and Belgian sections followed Bakunin on his expulsion at the 1872 Hague Congress; and when the General Council decided, at Geneva in 1873, to move to New York, the French Blanquists walked out. The Association dissolved after the Philadelphia Congress of July 1876. The Second International was formed only in 1889.

There was no party or group surviving from the Commune which could carry on underground propaganda against the reaction. This fact, which had led to the undoing of the Commune, equally prevented its perpetuation in political or agitational form. As after 1848, it was a time for reflection, for the slow gathering of proletarian forces for the next stage in the struggle.

It was not until twenty years later that Guesde and Jaurès revived the working-class movement in France; and here, as elsewhere in Europe, it left the revolutionary line laid down for it in the 'sixties. That this was so was due in some measure to the Commune, although it was primarily so conditioned by the French capitalist recovery, for which most of the political credit is due to Thiers.

While the Communards rot in New Caledonia, starve in Camden Town, yawn in Zürich, whisper in the broken streets of Belleville, the scene changes to Versailles and the provincial platforms and the inner offices of the great banks.

The transition from Empire to Republic merely represented in political form the readjustment of economic forces which, released and promoted by the *coup d'état* of 1851, had obtained virtual control of the Empire by about 1864, and began to assume political power openly after 1868. The Bordeaux elections of 1871 had been fought on the issue of peace, not of constitutional or social reform. The Royalist success did not mean, and was not intended to mean, a serious attempt at Royalist restoration, but simply an affirmation of provincial Conservatism. Royalism had ceased to be the expression of any important economic interest or grouping; and it could only have been imposed by a *coup d'état* which would have lacked the mass-support that enabled Louis Napoléon to survive the first difficult years after his seizure of power.

The Royalists did not disappear without a struggle.

In its early days the Third Republic was haunted by a fear of reactionary counter-revolution which has left its mark on its present constitution. Politically, the threat failed for three reasons; the pure stupidity of the Royalists themselves, the opposition of large bodies of provincial opinion which had formerly tended towards Orleanism, and the supreme vanity-inspired strategy of Adolphe Thiers.

The Commune had given the bourgeois in the provinces time for reflection. The conduct of the Bordeaux Assembly had shown up Royalism in its true colours. Bad as the Commune had seemed,

the rule of the Versailles "backwoodsmen" appeared far worse.
Thiers had rallied big business and the middle classes by proving that the Republic was strong enough to smash its "lunatic
fringe" and to keep order; that it had the army as well as the
police to defend it. He had proved, even more importantly, that
his Republic had no intention whatever of altering the social re-
lations which had made, supported and broken the Empire.

Gambetta, no less opportunist than Thiers, played into his
enemy's hands by rallying the petty-bourgeoisie, that class incapable of making its own political decisions, to reformism and
nationalism. He declared that "the heroic age is over"; he was
prepared, even as early as July 1871, to co-operate in restoring
Thiers's "moral order," endowed with "the necessary liberties"
in order to prepare La Révanche against Prussia. The policy won
the Republic 100 seats of 111 at the by-elections of July 2, 1871,
and laid the foundations of the overwhelming importance in
French politics of the grocer, the rentier, the small peasant and
all those elements which now adhere to the Radical Party.

Thiers had thus tricked his enemy into supporting him. He had
done what he could to prevent the Republic from "opening a
fair field to the working class for the struggle for its own interests, and, in any case, bringing matters to a crisis by which
the nation would be fairly and irresistibly launched in the revolutionary career, or else the status quo before the Revolution
restored as nearly as possible, and, thereby, a new revolution ren-
dered unavoidable" (Engels). Democracy, as Thiers boasted, had
indeed been "bled for a generation."

Gambetta and the Left were forced into a policy of pure opportunism. He raised the new formula of "National Union." "Let
us," he said, "return to the fertile ideas of 1789, restore the cor-
poration ["faisceau," the Italian "fascio"] destroyed by criminals:
the union of bourgeois with worker, of worker with peasant."
This appeal to the "new strata" achieved its final effect in Wal-
deck-Rousseau's National Unity Cabinet in 1899, when the Socialist Millerand took his seat beside the Versaillese killer, Marquis de Galliffet.

The Royalists aided Thiers by comitting political suicide as
neatly and ostentatiously as possible with the manifestos of the
Comte de Chambord, couched in terms so fatal that there was a

current suspicion that one of Thier's *agents-provocateur* must have inspired them. They finally alienated the provincial towns, who transferred their loyalty to Conservative Republicanism.

Thiers knew well enough that the Assembly was clay in his hands after the defeat of the Commune. He manœuvred them— "150 insurgents and 400 poltroons"—into voting their constituent power to save their own existence, and to do so by a vote of confidence in their detested leader. On August 31, 1871, after a day of stormy intrigue, the Assembly voted itself Constituent by 434 votes to 225: and by 491 to 94 the Royalist body declared Adolphe Thiers first President of the Third Republic, but only for the duration of the Assembly. Thiers had founded the Republic in spite of the Republicans.

The Republic was not finally constituted as the Government of France until January 30, 1875, and then only by the accidental majority of one vote.

Thiers was not there to see it. The Assembly had thrown over its saviour one evening, May 24, 1873, and the old Marshal Mac-Mahon, Royalist at heart, but more strongly attached to his own dictatorship, had been elected President for seven years.

The Septennate favoured all the Monarchist interests without restoring the Monarch. It suppressed opposition papers, introduced espionage in factory and home, revived clericalism, rejected every motion for an amnesty for the Communards. It encouraged the building of the Sacred Heart as an "expiation for the crimes of the Commune."[2]

The amnesty proclaimed its fall, the swing from reaction to opportunism. The Communards were pardoned at last on July 10, 1880. Galliffet wrote to Gambetta that it had made a deplorable impression upon the army. The Republic had still to submit to this form of political blackmail.

Owing to these peculiar political conditions, the immediate effect of the Commune appeared rather in the superstructural region of thought and philosophy. Sensitive and representative thinkers were horrified. Taine, who had begun his vast *History of Contemporary France* (published 1875-94) amid the roar of the Commune's guns, abandoned his *esprit geometrique* for the

[2] More generally known as the Church of the Sacré-Cœur. (Editor's note.)

refuge of the *esprit de finesse*. The horror was inexplicable, man simply a "lubricious gorilla."

Flaubert, who had declared the creed of the 'sixties as the "faith in science, the idea, the peaceful and sincere study of nature and reality," could not recover from the Commune's "Gothicity." He who had so objectively described, in *Education Sentimentale*, the collapse of society in 1848, relapsed into ferocious self-parody in *Bouvard et Pécuchet*, from which it was but a step to the madhouse.

Renan, who had won his chair at the Collège de France only in 1870 in the teeth of the Emperor's hostility, a victory which had seemed the promise of intellectual freedom at last, relapsed into sterile pyrrhonism. His example, the flight to the Ivory Tower of sensualism or mysticism, was followed by those of the younger democrats, such as Anatole France and Catulle Mendès, as did not, like Gautier, Sarcey, Daudet and Dumas fils, simply disgrace themselves by the cold brutality of what they wrote about the Commune.

Even some military men, such as de Cissey's valued aide-de-camp, Colonel Hepp, buried themselves in the work of reorganising the army, and walked solitary in the woods in their leisure. They could never again be brought to mention the Battle of Paris.

In the course of time, the "canonising" tendency, which Lenin noted in the case of Marx, has been brought by the French bourgeoisie to bear upon the Communards. Many Paris streets now bear their names, and some of them are situated in the most "respectable" districts. There are the rues Antoine-Arnaud (XVI), J.-B. Clément (XVIII), Gustave-Courbet (XVI), Bénoit-Malon (XX), Edouard-Vaillant (XX), Jules-Vallès (XI), Eugène-Varlin (X), the Boulevard Auguste-Blanqui (XIII).

In 1934 a tablet was placed in Père-Lachaise in honour of the National Guards of the 55th and 120th Battalions killed at the surprise at Moulin-Saquet. It is beside the great memorial to the Commune, to which great pilgrimages of Paris workers march every Whit Sunday, the *Mur des Fédérés*.[3]

---

[3] Père-Lachaise, the famous cemetery, was the scene of the Communards' last stand, and many of them were executed against one of its walls. Hence, the *Mur des Fédérés*, the wall where members of the federated National Guards battalions died. (Editor's note.)

The bourgeois who hated, slandered and killed the Communards are now "forgiving" them. The Nationalist Léon Daudet has praised their "patriotism." The revolutionaries Clément, Courbet, Vaillant, Malon are conveniently forgotten in the balladist, painter, municipal reformer, Deputy. The Academy celebrated Jules Vallès' centenary in 1932.

On the other hand, tens of thousands of workers of all parties gathered in September 1932 to bury Camélinat, last surviving personal link between the First International, the Commune and the Third International. In the same month the Red Municipality of Saint-Denis "at last shot Thiers down the drain," as a Radical paper expressed it, by renaming the rue Thiers rue Degeyter, the composer of the music for the "International," the words of which were written by Eugène Pottier, member of the Commune.

The ultimate historical importance of the Commune is to be found, not in French social or political relationships, but in the domain of revolutionary theory.

The Commune was the first concrete example of a workers' seizure of power. The Commune was compelled, by force of circumstances, even more than by inclination, to adopt many of the forms of the proletarian dictatorship. At the same time, adverse circumstances, conflicting aims and tendencies and the general incoherence of the event made it fertile in examples of every revolutionary hypothesis. Thus the Commune became a valuable touchstone upon which the validity of every kind of revolutionary theory could be tested.

The two main questions raised during the theoretic struggles which occupied the years between 1889 and 1917 were: First, What was the real character of the State-form which the Commune had set up, and how far did it differ from the true Socialist workers' State? Second, Should the workers take the offensive immediately they are threatened, even though a revolutionary situation might not have fully developed, even though defeat be practically certain? In a word, Was the Commune too violent or not violent enough?

The course of this controversy, brought to a head by Lenin in his attack upon Plekhanov's "they should not have taken up arms" in 1905, lies outside the scope of this study. It is, however, worth repeating that Lenin based his *State and Revolution* (1917) directly upon Marx's interpretation of the Paris Commune; and that *State and Revolution* is the basis of the Marxist-Leninist theory which now exercises a direct or indirect influence upon an enormous proportion of the world's population. If any proof of a theory's validity lies in its concrete effect, the controversy based upon the practical experience of the Commune must be allowed a very important place indeed in world history.

The police or judicial interpretation must be, for practical purposes the final one, since it is the expression of the opinion of the State Executive. "No, gentlemen," replied Dufaure, the merciless Minister for Justice, to some Liberals who pleaded that the Commune was merely a rash but not unpardonable outburst of patriotic municipal exasperation; "no, gentlemen, it was not a communalist, a municipal movement; it was in its ideals and its actions the most radical revolution ever undertaken!"

There have been revolutions yet more radical since that of March 18, 1871. The Commune was only the first stage; the Russian October was the second. They are intimately linked, histrically and traditionally, in the minds of those workers of France who, in numbers yearly increasing, demand each Whit Sunday at the *Mur des Fèdérés "Les Soviets partout!"*[4]

[4] The old French Marxist cry, literally "Workers' Councils Everywhere!" Note again that Jellinek's history was first published in 1937. (Editor's note.)

2 FROM *M. Winock and J.-P. Azéma*
Non-Marxian French Socialist View

M. Winock (1937-   ) and J.-P. Azéma (1937-   ) have recently produced a small book on the Commune that represents the current views of French labor and non-Marxian socialism about the Commune.

SOURCE. M. Winock and J.-P. Azéma, *Les Communards*, Paris: Editions du Seuil, 1964, pp. 177–180. Translated for this book by Roger L. Williams. Copyright 1964 by Editions du Seuil. Reprinted by permission of Editions du Seuil and the authors.

They do not see the Communal government as a worker regime resolved to overturn a capitalist regime. Yet they see the Communard as the first revolutionary of the industrial age, expressing the hope for a radically new world, and the Commune as one of the greatest events in labor history.

In following the chronology of events, we are struck by the complexity of the causes for the Commune. It was first seen as an organized reply to the German invasion, a patriotic matter. The Communard, as time passed, was seen as a patriot angered by what he called "the treason" of the Government of National Defense, which was simply continued by the Thiers government that emerged from the February 8 elections. Political causes were also evident: the Communard was also the defender of the Republic, which was seriously in danger from the royalist majority in the National Assembly. The tension between a patriotic and Republican Paris, on the other hand, and a conservative and pacifist Assembly, on the other created the psychological conditions for an insurrection. Finally, the Commune had its social and economic causes: the sociological composition of Paris, the suffering during the siege, the various decisions of the Assembly in Bordeaux, and the jeopardized interests of the lower middle class, which joined its anger with that of the workers. Finally, the insurrection could take place because of the weakness of the Regular Army and the relative strength of the National Guard, which had escaped the control of the established government. The Communard was a fédéré [a member of the federated battalions comprising the National Guard]. Whatever the causes, the important thing was that a revolution was born and a new power took over.

We have used the term Communard to mean both the man at the Hôtel de Ville and the man in the street. They were jointly and separately liable, just as the voter and the deputy under parliamentary regimes are both responsible. At the same time, it is proper to point out distinctions. If we agree with the Marxist writings that the Communards of the street were overwhelmingly workers (or more precisely artisans), we can still object to the notion that the Communards of the Hôtel de Ville established a "worker government."

It is a fact that the Communal government included a number of workers who had never before participated in a government, but they were hardly among the Majority. Were the remainder [of the members] for the most part "the recognized leaders of the working class?" On May 13, 1871, Marx himself wrote to Frankel and to Varlin: "We note that influences other than those of the workers still remain [in the Commune]." Let us not forget that as a group the Jacobins formed the largest single faction and that they represented by and large a part of the middle class, so much so that labor interests did not seem to be their immediate concern.

Whatever its composition, did the Commune government proceed in the manner of a worker government? Was it, according to Engels' expression, the first "dictatorship of the proletariat?" One would have difficulty proving it. The supporters of a dictatorship were not lacking, but they were the men farthest from the people and the least ready to take practical measures to provide the social emancipation of the workers. As for those who represented the proletariat more directly, the members of the International in particular, they were, with one or two exceptions, opposed to dictatorship in any form. In Marxist writings, the ideas of the Minority are too often juggled, probably because their source was Proudhon and Bakunin. The greater part of these workers in the Hôtel de Ville were inclined to the "anarchist" lines (autonomy, federalism, and collectivism), which ran counter to the centralism that Marx and Lenin believed to be necessary to destroy the power of the bourgeoisie.

Moreover, we cannot discern in the Communal movement any conscious or systematic desire to destroy capitalism. At most, only a few hints may be discerned in various pieces of legislation. In the Commune's *faux pas*, in its hesitations, its indecision, its scruples, one can see—even more than in the formal debates—the lack of class consciousness.

Nor do we believe that a case can be made for greater [class] awareness on the part of those in the streets. Those in the Hôtel de Ville were not sufficiently concerned for the opinions expressed in the popular clubs, thus did not really rely on popular strength; the latter for their part, despite their sane reaction against the extremism of some of the elected members, never succeeded in imposing their strength or their will upon the Hôtel de Ville.

Such limitations, however, do not deprive the Revolution of '71 and its work from having a singularly new character. As Marx said, a new state had come into being. Suddenly, the word *democracy* was no longer mere rhetoric. Everyone had the right to speak, the right to censure, the right to criticize! Not only were these *rights* given to the masses, but by their spontaneous activities, the people gave the new regime a new quality, a new tone. This was both a revolution of their expectations and of their thoughtlessness. Better yet, frontiers were done away with by this popular gladness. Among the crowd that applauded the destruction of the Vendôme column were Poles, Belgians, and Italians, joining the shouting with the Parisians, just as they would soon also shed their blood with them. Whether at the Hôtel de Ville, in the street, or in the fighting, the Communard was a citizen of the universal Republic.

3 FROM *Jacques Chastenet*
Moderate Conservative View

Jacques Chastenet de Castaing (1893-) has had a long career in letters, journalism, and business, writing numerous histories that have culminated in his multi-volume history of the Third Republic from which this extract is taken. A Parisian by birth, he is also a wine-grower in the Gironde. Having been decorated for both military and intellectual merit by Britain, Portugal, and France, he was elected to the Académie des sciences morales et politiques *in 1947, and to the*

SOURCE. Jacques Chastenet, *Histoire de la Troisième République, L'Enfance de la Troisieme, 1870–1879,* Paris: Hachette, 1952, Vol. I, pp. 104–106. Translated for this book by Roger L. Williams. Copyright 1952 by Librairie Hachette. Reprinted by permission of Librairie Hachette and the author.

Académie française *in 1956. He has been a man of letters rather than a professor, and represents the moderate or conservative Republican tradition.*

It has been estimated that between 17,000 and 20,000 Parisians fell in the course of the Bloody Week. (The Terror, during the Great Revolution, had no more than 12,000 victims in all of France; and not until the troubled days of 1944 would France again experience comparable fratricide.)

But the repression did not stop with the defeat of the insurrection. Patrols roamed the streets without warrants, houses were searched, and arrests made. Newspapers could be published only with permission of the military authorities. Until June 3, one had to have a pass either to enter or to leave Paris. But on that day, theaters were reopened, and a crowd of English, led by travel agencies, hastened to the capital to gape at the smoking ruins. On June 6, Edmond de Goncourt would write in his *Journal* "Reappearance of the crowd on the pavement of the Boulevard des Italiens, deserted a few days ago. This evening, for the first time, one begins to have difficulty weaving a path between the sauntering of the men and the prostitution of the women."

For several days, interminable lines of prisoners filled the roads to Versailles where the wretched creatures, numbering about 36,000, were crammed either into the Satory camp or into hastily improvised camps under the worst conditions, before being removed to either Brest, Lorient, Cherbourg, Rochefort, or La Rochelle. Some summary executions took place with the pretext that the victims had attempted to escape and some with no pretext at all. Then justice became more regularized. Twenty-two courts-martial were established, which would sit until the end of 1875, hearing and pronouncing on 46,835 cases. Of these, roughly 13,000 were found guilty [including those *in absentia*] and given sentences that ranged from death to banishment, forced labor, deportation to New Caledonia, or to simple imprisonment. It must be said that of the two hundred sentenced to death, only twenty-six were executed.

As so often happens, the minor players found themselves

hardest hit. Of the seventy-nine members of the Commune as of May 21, only one, Delescluze, died on the barricades. Two of them, Jacques Durand and Raoul Rigault were shot during the Bloody Week, as was Varlin, although he had earlier resigned his seat. Four members, including the courageous Rossel, were shot by virtue of courtmartial verdicts. The remainder more or less got out of it. Instead, it would soon seem—whether from summary executions, imprisonment, death through privation in the camps, or from voluntary exile—that half the house painters, roofers, zinc workers, plumbers, and shoemakers of Paris had disappeared.

The victory of Order achieved, a heavy silence fell on the capital where the rubbish of so many monuments, of so many houses still smoked, where gaping wounds could be seen in many façades, where many streets were either obstructed by the remains of barricades or still suffering the loss of their paving stones.

Those insurgents who had managed to avoid death or arrest took cover and were silent, feeling the reprobation of France mounting against them. In the Assembly at Versailles, not one voice, not even from the pillars of the Left, was raised to appeal for clemency. Two amnesty proposals would be presented, one in September of 1871, the other in July of 1872, by Henri Brisson and by Louis Blanc; but they rallied no response, and it would be necessary to wait nine years until another Assembly, after a heated appeal from Gambetta, decided to remove the last remnants of the civil war with a bill of complete oblivion.[1]

In a material way, Paris recovered quickly from the blow given her. She would be a very long time recovering morally, perhaps never entirely recovering. She had been deeply wounded, not only in body but in spirit. The vitality in her had been injured, a pride brought down, a faith extinguished. She could again become the political capital of France, [but only by submitting to the rural majorities in Parliament], and she would raise no more barricades (except seventy-three years later against the German occupant). Still patriotic, indeed chauvinistic, she would cease to be revolutionary and would often appear to be even

[1] While a pardon is granted to an individual as an act of forgiveness, an amnesty erases the deed or the crime. Hence, the amnesty bill of 1880 was one of "complete oblivion." (Editor's note.)

more "to the Right" than the rest of the country. To find echos of her past passions, you would have to go beyond her limits into the new "red belt." Even so, the turner or the fitter of Saint-Denis or of Villeneuve-Saint-Georges would be a far different man from the old artisan of Belleville or of the faubourg Saint-Antoine.

More generally, the Commune notably retarded that social progress that had been one of its goals. "As for socialism," Flaubert wrote . . . , "it will be dead for a long time." Speaking at Le Havre on April 18, 1872, Gambetta declared: "There is no social question!" And in his profession of faith of 1877, which became his testament, Thiers would write: "No one speaks of socialism any more, and that is good. We are rid of socialism." Reform projects to improve the lot of the downtrodden would long suffer from the memory of the Tuileries in flames, of murdered hostages. To an appreciable degree, the Second Empire had been concerned for the workers. Many years would have to pass before the Third Republic would think of them, and the British and German monarchies would be less timid about [social reform] than she.

Politics alone counted. To be "advanced," first of all, was to be anticlerical—and hardly anything more than that. Even among the democrats, the social issues seemed suspect; and the First International did not long survive its part, hesitating though it may have been, in the Parisian insurrection. The Communist Party may endeavor to celebrate the Commune as a notable date in proletarian history, but that date in fact marked a lasting setback. How true it is that well-being cannot spring from destruction, and that hatred, which only breeds hatred, was never more prolific.

4 FROM *Alfred Cobban*
Liberal View

Alfred Cobban (1901-1967) has been one of the most distinguished students of French history in our time. Although a specialist in eighteenth-century politics and thought, his grasp of wider problems has been impressive. Trained at Cambridge, his ultimate academic appointment was as Professor of French History at University College, London. He has also been serving as editor of History. *His interpretation of the Commune is one of the contemporary liberal interpretations: non-Marxist, but inclined to sympathy for the Communards.*

France invariably looks to those it has known for many years when a national crisis emerges. Nevertheless, an overwhelmingly monarchist assembly had begun by placing in the key positions two republicans; and Thiers' three leading ministers, Favre, Picard, and Simon, were also republicans.

But there was more than one kind of republican in the minority of the Assembly. Paris had sent a group of deputies, including Louis Blanc, Victor Hugo, Delescluze, Ledru-Rollin, Rochefort, Quinet, whose names were like a roll-call of '48. To the monarchist majority they were intolerable and in fact were so little tolerated that some eight of them resigned. The National Assembly, under the leadership of Thiers, was determined to eliminate the danger from the left, and now this meant almost exclusively Paris. A court martial sentenced Blanqui and Flourens, as leaders of the 31 October rising, to death in their absence. The former Bonapartist, d'Aurelle de Paladines, dismissed by Gambetta, was put in command of the Paris National Guard. The Assembly was

SOURCE. Alfred Cobban, *A History of Modern France*, Baltimore: Penguin Books, 1961, Vol. II, pp. 206–210. Reprinted by permission of Penguin Books Ltd. Copyright 1961 by Alfred Cobban.

brought back from Bordeaux to Versailles instead of to Paris. Finally, Thiers gave orders for the 400 guns in the hands of the National Guard of Paris to be removed on 18 March. It has been described as a deliberate provocation, which Thiers never expected to succeed in any other respect; but he did not expect his troops from Versailles to fraternize with the Parisians, and he expected the National Guard from the middle-class quarters of Paris to give his policy support. This was to underestimate the effect of two fatal measures passed by the Assembly. The first had ended the moratorium on the promissory notes through which much of the business of Paris was conducted; the second was to make rents which had remained unpaid during the war immediately payable. These decisions seemed very reasonable to the landed gentry of the Assembly, to the financiers who had speculated in paper and rents, and to Thiers. They spelt ruin to the lower middle classes of Paris.

Thiers' attempted seizure of the guns was the spark which set off revolution in Paris. After a riot and a few murders, he ordered the abandonment of Paris by all the legal authorities. The only organized body left in the city was the moderate Central Committee of the National Guard, which found itself obliged to take over the essential services, abandoned by Thiers' orders. Naturally those who came to the front in this emergency were the stronger and extremer leaders, bred in the red clubs which had flourished during the siege of Paris. The eternal conspirator, Blanqui, temporarily not the eternal prisoner, had been the inspiring genius of the most famous of the clubs, meeting in the Halles. His *club rouge* had been described as 'a chapel consecrated to an orthodox classical cult of conspiracy, in which the doors were wide open to everyone, but to which one only returned if one was a convert'. Blanqui himself presided over the cult, with 'his delicate, superior, calm countenance, his narrow, piercing eyes shot across now and again with a dangerous, sinister light'—an unusually favourable picture of the conspirator described by Victor Hugo as 'a sort of baleful apparition in whom seemed to be incarnated all the hatred born of every misery'.

The Blanquists were only a tiny fraction, the rest of the Parisian rebels felt the need to legitimize their position by holding elections. A municipal government, to be known by the historic but alarming name of Commune, was elected on 26 March. The name of the Commune was a memory of the year II, of the Jacobins of Robespierre and the *sans-culottes* of Hébert. It was a symbol beneath which the most opposed schools of revolutionary thought could rally. Four separate groups can be distinguished among its members—the pure revolutionaries, divided between Blanquists and Jacobins, the federalists following Proudhon, and the adherents of the First International. The conservatives or moderates returned in the first election of the Commune resigned, and after complementary elections there was a revolutionary majority of some 57 Blanquists and Jacobins, and a socialist and Proudhonist minority of about 22.

It is a mistake to regard the Commune as Marxist in inspiration; only one of its members can be described as a Marxist. Equally it was not a government of the working-class. Though there were 25 *ouvriers*, there were more than twice as many lesser bourgeois or professional men. The 'Declaration to the French People' issued by the Commune on 19 April represents the federalist tendencies of the minority. As soon as the active struggle began, the Blanquists, weakened by the absence of their prophet, who had been arrested and returned to jail as soon as danger began to threaten in Paris, and the Jacobins, headed by Delescluze, took control in a temporary alliance, to be followed, as in 1793, by bitter quarrels. On 1 May they set up a Committee of Public Safety by 45 votes to 23.

The second siege of Paris began on Palm Sunday, 2 April, by a Versailles army in a wretched state of disorganization and lack of materiel and morale. Its first military achievement was to shoot five prisoners. The forces of the Commune retaliated with a wild sortie in the direction of Versailles, which was easily dispersed with the loss of some 1,000 prisoners captured by the Versaillais, who picked out those they thought were the leaders and shot them. Given a small measure of capacity and unity, at the outset the Commune should have been able to take the offensive with success. It had many more men and guns than Versailles, and a base in the fortified camp of Paris which could be provisioned through the neutral Prussian lines. These advantages were gradually lost. While the leaders of the Commune talked and small bodies of men defended the forts, the life of Paris, theatres, concerts, the busy traffic of the streets, went on much as usual and far more normally than during the Prussian siege. Such changes as were deliberately debated and brought about by the Commune were hardly of major importance. The old revolutionary calendar was revived and May 1871 became *floréal* year LXXIX. The Vendôme column was pulled down in a great public ceremony.

Meanwhile the military strength of Versailles was growing. On 8 May a general bombardment of the fortifications began. The forts round the south of Paris, gallantly defended by isolated groups of men, fell one by one. On 21 May a section of the walls near the porte de Saint-Cloud was discovered to be undefended, and by nightfall the Versaillais had a large body of men within Paris. On the same day the Commune held its last official meeting, devoted typically to a trial of its own military commander. Both he and his successor had failed to secure a reasonable measure of military behaviour from the forces of the Commune. Now that Paris was at bay, the old Jacobin Delescluze proclaimed a war of the people, not conducted by staff officers and military discipline, but by the people, the *bras-nus*. And now that all was really lost the Communards at last began to fight in earnest, in the traditional way, the only way that the people of Paris knew. It was a street battle of barricades, which was the rage for seven days across the breadth of Paris from west to east.

The Versaillais, strong in the knowledge that they were defending order and public morality, throughout the fighting showed more barbarity than the Communards. Apart from the initial episode and the actual fighting, there were practically no shootings of opponents or suspected opponents in Paris until the last stages were reached, though hostages were seized. The Versaillais systematically shot their prisoners. This was one motive of the subsequent murders of hostages that accompanied the final battle in the streets of Paris; but also, it is true, there was a group of ruthless men among the leaders of the Commune, who had not distinguished themselves in the fighting but had had their eye on the hostages all the time. Now they had their chance and particularly chose priests, including the Archbishop of Paris, for their victims. To the horror of the street fighting and massacres on both sides was added fire. Incendiary shells from the Versaillais, the burning of buildings by the Communards to clear lines of fire or form a barrier destroyed much. The Tuileries and other public buildings were fired in a last act of defiance by desperate men, though the story of the *pétroleuses* is a mere piece of propaganda.[1]

In its final phase the defence of the Commune degenerated into uncoordinated episodes of heroism or cruelty. Delescluze, in the dress of a deputy of '48, top hat, frock coat, and red sash, cane in hand, all being now lost, mounted a barricade to be shot. The last combat of any size was among the graves of the Cemetery of Père-Lachaise; and there, on the next day, against the wall that was to become a place of pilgrimage, 147 Communards were shot. Military justice continued to take its toll. The Versaillese lost about 1,000 dead in the fighting; the death roll of the Communards was probably not less than 20,000. Thiers had won a notable victory in the class war; the illusions of 1789 and 1792 had drawn the people of Paris into the bloodiest and most merciless of all its defeats; the Second Empire had ended in disgraceful surrender, revolution and repression, blood and tears; but it was an assembly of monarchists, under a conservative republican head of state, that first provoked and then put to fire and sword the people of Paris. It is a mistake to say that the repression of the Commune founded the Third Republic. That was founded in the attempt to undo the evil that accompanied the end of the Second Empire.

[1] *Les Pétroleuses* were bands of female arsonists. For a contrary view, see a recent study on women in the Commune by E. Thomas, *Les Pétroleuses*, published in 1963. (Editor's note.)

5   FROM   *Sir Denis W. Brogan*
                Liberal View

*Sir Denis William Brogan (1900-   ) has written extensively on
American as well as on French political and historical problems.
Known both for his learning and for his elegant literary style, he has
been decorated by the French and the Dutch governments, and was
knighted by the Queen in 1963. He is Professor of Political Science
at Cambridge University and has been Visiting Professor at Harvard.
This brief account of the Commune reveals both Brogan's historical
skill and his liberal position.*

The armistice was a defeat for Paris even more than for France.
There were plenty of zealots in the city who still believed in the
magic of the Republic and there were others who agreed with
Gambetta that the Assembly, with which alone Bismarck would
make peace, must not include former Imperialist officials, Bismarck would have none of it; the new Assembly must consist
of those whom the French people freely chose.

Their choice at first sight was startling. The new Assembly was
overwhelmingly Royalist and Catholic. To the credulous, it
might seem that France had at last repented of her sins, had
turned both from the usurping Empire and anti-Catholic Republic to the cause of Church and King. The reality was very
different. Everywhere, the Republic was associated with war and
defeat. The French people voted for peace and, with the Imperial
political personnel discredited if not excluded, it turned to other
natural leaders, above all to the local gentry. The squires had
fought well; one of the heroic names of the war was that of the

SOURCE. Denis W. Brogan, *The French Nation from Napoleon to Pétain,
1814–1940*, New York: Harper Colophon, 1963, pp. 151–157. Copyright ©
1957 by D. W. Brogan. Reprinted by permission of Harper & Row, Publishers and the author.

'Chouan' general, Charette, with his banner of the Sacred Heart. But the Royalists were now the peace party. Voting by departments, for hastily composed lists, the mass of the electors made sure of peace by voting for the lists that had fewest notoriously Republican names. Where they could, they voted for Thiers; he was returned in thirty-two departments. The true-blue Republicans were only a hundred in a house of over seven hundred.

Before the election, the Republicans had preached the constituent power of the Assembly; now they declared, truly enough, that the only mandate the electors had given was for peace. The victors, who had not, except in a few instances, made any profession of political faith, claimed that the whole power of giving France new and reformed institutions lay with the Assembly which the people, in a possibly fleeting moment of wisdom, had chosen. But there were other things to be done first. Peace had to be made with Germany, peace involving the agonizing mutilation of the loss of Alsace-Lorraine. The deputies from the lost provinces protested in a moving scene. The Mayor of Strasbourg died of shock. But although Thiers saved the fortress of Belfort, Bismarck would make no further territorial concessions. The new provinces were his gift of joyous advent to the new Empire, a gift paid for at a terrible price, more than once, by France, by Germany, by Europe. The occupation of Paris was formal; but the east of France was to be held until the indemnity of £200,-000,000 was paid, an immense sum by the standards of that age. Financially as well as territorially, the war had paid a handsome profit to the victors, for the indemnity was really a ransom.

The armistice, the terms of the treaty, the personality of the head of the new Government, Thiers, the man of the Rue Transnonain,[1] the threat of a Royal Restoration were all salt rubbed in the wounds of Paris. There was, in fact, no immediate danger of a Royal Restoration. Thiers was theoretically a Royalist of the Orléanist stripe. He had had many harsh words to say of the bad habits of the Republic; he had kind words for the monarchists and even for the monarchy. But he insisted that first things must come first, and the National Assembly, meeting at Bordeaux,

[1] The scene of a massacre of Parisian workers by troops in the time of the July Monarchy. Thiers was popularly, and unfairly, held responsible as he was then Minister of the Interior. (Editor's note.)

accepted what was called 'the pact of Bordeaux'. Until peace was made and the most terribly urgent business settled, there was to be no upsetting of the provisional regime, the rule of 'the Chief of the Executive Power'.

Its bitter business done at Bordeaux, the Assembly moved, but not to feared, hated Paris. It moved to Versailles where it proceeded to legislate for and against the sullen city at its door. To the majority of the Assembly, Paris was the curse of France. To the majority of Parisians, the Assembly was a usurping group of squires, chosen by priest-ridden peasantry, representative of that rural France that had supported the Empire and failed to rescue Paris. It *was* largely a rural Assembly, and it failed to understand either the pride or the needs of Paris. The Paris National Guard was, to one faction, a permanent centre of disorder, of atheism, of socialism. To the majority of Parisians, it was the safeguard of the Republic, betrayed once, in danger of being betrayed again.

The Paris which drifted into revolt was not an industrial city of the modern proletarian type. As Sir John Clapham pointed out, it lacked the very basis of the new factory economy, power-driven machinery. There were true proletarians of the classical type in the railway yards; there were a few mass-production industries like the plate factories of the popular jeweller, Christophle. But Paris was a city of craftsmen, of shopkeepers, of servants, of officials, of clerks. All were affected by two stupid and unfeeling decisions of the Assembly—to end the moratorium on commercial bills passed in the last days of the Empire, and to end the suspension of house rents. Bills played a great part in the economic life even of minor businesses; few Parisians owned their flats or houses. Few but the rich had any funds either to pay their rent or to meet their other obligations. There was mass unemployment. As Millière foresaw, the situation of June 1848 had returned. But there were differences. The National Guard was more numerous, better armed, more combative. The Government was far weaker, dependent on very raw recruits and with a country too exhausted to display the enthusiasm for the restoration of order that had marked the rural National Guard in 1848. Tact, skill, sympathy were needed and were not at hand.

The National Guard of 1871 was better armed than that of

1848 in one very important way. It had its great artillery park
on the top of the semi-rural hill of Montmartre. Thiers decided
that it must be seized. The attempt failed and on March 18, the
Government found itself defeated and believed itself forced to
leave Paris. The great, heroic disaster of 'the Commune' began.

The Commune is more important as a legend than as an event,
bloody and materially destructive as it was. It was erected by
Marx in a brilliant pamphlet (*The Civil War in France*) into a
symbol and an example of what to do and what not to do. It
provoked the execration of all right-thinking people and the
more or less covert sympathies of the Left everywhere, sympathies that grew bolder and more open as their expression became less dangerous. It was not a proletarian and still less a
Marxian revolt. The only leader who knew anything of Marxism
was the Hungarian Jew, Fränkel. It expressed agonizing patriotic
frustration and the illusions and despairs of the old revolutionary
tradition much more than any socialist or communist convictions.
Marx had warned the French workers at the time of the over-
throw of the Empire that their business was 'not to begin the past
over again, but to build the future'. And certainly one of the
numerous and fatal errors of the Commune was its passion for
reviving the traditions of the Revolution.

The name 'Commune of Paris' had all the implications of the
great Commune of Paris that had overthrown Louis XVI. Since
there had been a 'Committee of Public Safety' in 1793, there must
be one in 1871. Since Hébert had published his *Père Duchesne*
under the old Commune, there must be a vulgar, obscene and
tedious imitation of it under the new. There was no unified
revolutionary doctrine. For some Danton was a hero; for others
Robespierre; for others Chaumette and Hébert. The ineffable
Félix Pyat, the most imbecile of the leaders, used Mignet's tepid
Histoire de la Révolution Française as a handbook. The sacred
revolutionary institution of the political club was revived; there
was a 'Club des Folies Bergère', a 'Club du Collège de France'.
(These very different institutions played the part of the original
Jacobins and Cordeliers in giving their names to the politicians
who used their premises.) There were political cafés like La
Corderie du Temple. There was endless talk and declamation

with messages from political painters like Courbet, Bohemian men of letters like Jules Vallès, innocent well-wishers to mankind like Beslay. There were Jacobin doctrinaires like Delescluze, disciples of Blanqui like Vaillant (Blanqui was held as a hostage by the Government of Versailles). But there was no party, no doctrine, no plan of campaign, military or political. Nor was there, at first, any very resolute revolutionary intention. Many left-wing deputies hoped to arrange some kind of patched-up peace, to let tempers cool. Thiers and the majority of the Assembly, but above all Thiers, were determined that, once and for all, Paris should be taught a lesson. Thiers had always thought that the way to deal with a rebellious Paris was to besiege it and capture it in a great military operation. He was determined to try his recipe now. There was blood already between the Assembly and Paris, for the mob on Montmartre had murdered Generals Lecomte and Clément Thomas despite the efforts of the Mayor of Montmartre, the younger Dr. Clemenceau. Willy-nilly, 'the Commune' was forced to fight.

What was the Commune? It was represented by Thiers and his allies as a body of secret conspirators, an agency of that mysterious body 'the International', whose numbers, power, unity were fantastically exaggerated. The real authority of the 'Commune' was the delegates of 'the Republican Federation of the National Guard', a body that gave the misleading name of 'Fédérés' to the soldiers of the Commune. Not all of the National Guard accepted the authority of the 'Central Executive Committee'. The Ist and VIth arrondissements were no more revolutionary then than now. Many of the more prosperous Parisians had fled Paris at the beginning of the siege. Others had left it after the armistice. Paris was more a city of the poor than it had ever been. The expulsion of the 'Versaillais', as the agents of the legal Government were beginning to be called, created some of the same credulous enthusiasm that had marked the Fourth of September. The people of that classic hotbed of revolution, Belleville, were told, 'You are the admiration of the world and it is Belleville that will save Europe.' On March 26, a municipal council was elected which took the august name of 'the Commune of Paris', inspiring or terrifying according to taste. But the National Guard officers did not abdicate and there was never anything like the Jacobin, still less the Bolshevik unity of command.

Had the Commune advanced on Versailles at once, it might have driven out Thiers from his stronghold. But it had no revolutionary programme. It hoped (as Paris had hoped) that the provinces would come to its rescue; but apart from a few verbal demonstrations in the Midi, France lay passive, Bismarck hastened the return of enough soldiers of the old Army to give Thiers the means of crushing the revolt; a great sortie failed; its leaders were shot. There was more blood. Paris was again invested except in the section commanded by the scornful Germans. Inside Paris, dreams were the order of the day. Generals were appointed, defeated, deposed. The National Guard displayed very uneven zeal in guarding the walls. The key fortress of Mont-Valérien, hastily abandoned by the Versaillais, had been hastily re-occupied. There was no hope for the Commune. In vain it issued proclamations, organized patriotic demonstrations, abolished the union of Church and State, pursued with irrelevant zeal priests and nuns. Its only social legislation was the abolition of night work in bakeries. It respected the sacred autonomy of the Bank of France from which it borrowed money in due, bourgeois form. It was a pageant rather than a revolution.

But each day, the power of Versailles grew. As the end cast its shadow before, sinister figures like Raoul Rigault, disciple more of the Marquis de Sade than of Robespierre or Condorcet, came to the top. Hostages were seized—the liberal Archbishop of Paris, the President of the Court of Cassation. Treachery opened one of the gates, and slowly the avenging troops of Versailles entered Paris. They had much to avenge: Sedan and Metz as well as the atrocities freely attributed to the 'Communards'. There were legends of viragos with bottles of petrol—the 'petroleuses'—to inflame them. The maniacal elements of the Commune took command. A great part of Paris, the Tuileries, the Hôtel-de-Ville, the Cour des Comptes, went up in flames. In Basle, Burckhardt heard, with horror, that the Louvre had been destroyed. It was saved by its keeper, Héron de Villefosse; but it was by the light of the devastating fires set by the Communards that the victorious restorers of order worked. The hostages were slain. Archbishop Darboy died like his two immediate predecessors by violence. Paris was a see as dangerous as nineteenth-century Korea or medieval Canterbury.

Vengeance was exacted on a colossal scale. What was to be called 'the bloody week' was the bloodiest in the bloody history of Paris. At least 20,000 perished at the hands of the forces of order. Some leaders, like the upright Varlin, were shot after farcical courts martial; Delescluze, the last of the Jacobins, died, in the great tradition, on the barricades, girt with his tricolour sash. But most victims of the victors were shot out of hand. The final battle took place in the cemetery of Père Lachaise. There, before what was to be known as the 'mur des Fédérés', which became another of those shrines of bloody memory in which Paris is too rich, the Commune died.

Thiers had won; he had tamed Paris. Never again did it decide the fate of France. The respectable world rejoiced, although Matthew Arnold knew too well what Thiers stood for to find his victory heartwarming. The fine ladies of Versailles, who had seen Paris burning from the terraces, screamed for more blood. The execution squads were busy. 'Blood was on the grass like dew.' The last word was to a boy of genius who had escaped from the doomed city. The triumph of the frightened bourgeoisie made Rimbaud vomit:

> 'O cœurs de saleté, bouches épouvantables,
> Fonctionnez plus fort, bouches de puanteurs,
> Un vin, pour ces torpeurs ignobles, sur ces tables!
> Vos ventres sont fondus de hontes, vainqueurs.'[2]

The Commune was a folly; some of its leaders were criminals. But the greatest crime of its authors (of whom Thiers was one) was in making final that alienation of the workers of Paris from the official organization of the French State which the days of June 1848 had begun. The 'bloody week' of May 1871 was a wound that, if at times it seemed closed, was never really healed.

[2] Oh hearts of filthiness, ugly mouths,
  Grind on, mouths full of stink,
  Let there be wine on these tables for that vile apathy!
  Your bellies burst with infamies, Conquerers.

6 FROM   *David Thomson*
                      Liberal View

David Thomson (1912-   , of Sidney Sussex College, Cambridge,
since 1948, has also been in residence at Columbia University and
at the Institute for Advanced Study at Princeton. His distinguished
publications have centered on French and British history in the nine-
teenth and twentieth centuries. The following extract really supple-
ments the previous reading, representing the same contemporary
liberal point of view but giving a more sympathetic appraisal of
Thiers' role.

The relevance of the whole revolutionary tradition, with all
its nuances, to the operation of democratic ideas in the Third
Republic takes dramatic form in the episode of the Paris Commune. The Commune of 1871 caught up, fused and projected
forward into the new Republic every main strand in the revolutionary tradition. Confused and short-lived though it was, the
experience of the Commune provided the lurid and violent back-
ground against which the institutions of the Republic were de-
vised and consolidated. Seized upon by Marx and exalted, in his
pamphlet, into the model pattern and classical triumph of insur-
rectionary proletariat over centralized nation-State, it provided
the nascent Communist Party with a powerful new *mystique*. The
French revolutionary tradition, in its most violent form, was thus
adopted and borrowed by the most extreme Socialist movement
of the Republic. This transference had considerable significance
in later years: even though it rested on a confusion of *capitulards*
with *capitalistes, communards* with *communistes*.

SOURCE. David Thomson, *Democracy in France Since 1870*, fourth edition, New York: Oxford University Press, 1964, pp. 24–27. Reprinted by
permission of Oxford University Press and the author. Copyright 1958,
1964 by Royal Institute of International Affairs.

Historically, the Commune represented neither the theory nor the work of Marxism. Nor, of course, was it distinctively proletarian. It was the product of an immensely complex interaction of national and civic humiliation, economic distress and ideological aspirations. It began on 18 March 1871—after the national humiliation at Sedan, after Paris had endured four months' siege by the Germans, after Gambetta's republican Government of National Defence had failed to sustain the *guerre à outrance*, and after Bismarck's troops had marched down the Champs-Élysées. It was occasioned, but scarcely caused, by the decision of the new National Assembly at Bordeaux to move to Versailles rather than to Paris, and by the attempt of Thiers to remove the battery of guns from Montmartre. As an aftermath of the siege the population of Paris no longer included many of its more wealthy citizens, who had fled south, but it did include some 40,000 evacuees and refugees from the German-occupied provinces. The lead in the insurrection was taken by the few thousand followers of that peculiarly Parisian figure, Auguste Blanqui. His was the great name in the Paris underworld of full-time, professional revolutionaries which had grown up throughout the many changes of the nineteenth century. Blanqui's tradition was that of the barricades—he had fought behind them as early as 1827. He represents the simplest form of the revolutionary tradition, anti-parliamentarian and anarchist, and he was the idol of many young intellectuals. Perhaps he was the direct heir of Babeuf.[1]

Closely allied with the Blanquists in precipitating the Commune were the Jacobins, led by Delescluze and Félix Pyat. They clung to the old traditions, particularly deep-rooted in Paris, of the Commune of 1793 and the Reign of Terror. They kept as their slogans Liberty, Equality, Fraternity, Sovereignty of the People, and the Republic 'one and indivisible'. They had become long skilled in the technique of resistance in the previous fifty years but had become, in the process, quixotic, doctrinaire and romantic. These were the real *Communards*—harking back to the Terror as a golden age when republican virtue really triumphed, seeing

---

[1] Babeuf was an extremist of the 1790's, believing in economic equality at a time when equality was understood to mean political rights or opportunity. (Editor's note.)

in demagogy, an inflammatory press and the barricades the true instruments of progress. The spirit of Rousseau lived on, even in their 'city-State' conception of politics; and if these neo-Jacobins admitted an omnicompetent State, it was only the State as a commune, not as a nation.

To complete this apotheosis of the revolutionary tradition there were the Socialists—followers of Saint-Simon and Fourier, Louis Blanc himself and above all the disciples of Proudhon: uniting only in their demand for social reform or revolution to complete the political revolt. The disciples of Proudhon were particularly influential because his vision of society as a community of small, self-governing groups and co-operative associations glorified the Commune as the natural unit of society. To the extreme left the Communists, disciples of Marx and Engels, who played a considerable individual part in the history of the Commune. These included men like Édouard Vaillant, who became Minister of the Interior in the Commune: men like Leo Franckel who kept in touch with Marx himself, and with the First International which Marx had founded in 1864. As Professor Brogan has pointed out, 'Neither formally nor really had the International a leading role in the revolt, and . . . . it was not Marxism that was the animating creed of the Paris workers or their leaders.' The unanimity of the demand for 'a Commune' concealed a wide variety of different aims. 'The Commune' meant something different to each group, and provided the same sort of common rallying cry which the demand for 'a Constitution' provided in 1789, or for 'The Revolution' in Russia of 1917.

Marx, by adopting and defending the Commune in his manifesto of the International, later known as *The Civil War in France*, tried to make it the pattern for future proletarian revolutionary action. Considered historically, the Paris Commune makes sense only if it is regarded not as the hopeful model for future political action but as the somewhat forlorn climax of the old French tradition. It is an end rather than a beginning. For the next two generations, at least, the future was to lie with the big, centralized nation-State, and both political and technical developments were to militate against the success of local, spontaneous revolts. In a Europe where Germany and Italy had become political units, France too had to be a powerful central-

ized nation-State. In this sense Thiers ranks with Bismarck and
Cavour as one of the great nationalists of modern Europe. He
stood for the preservation of political and constitutional unity,
just as did his contemporary Abraham Lincoln in America: and
both had to fight a civil war in order to preserve union. The
Paris Commune was not the only revolt. Its example was followed
by other big cities—by Lyons, Marseilles, Saint-Étienne—and local
risings took place at Toulouse, Narbonne and Limoges. The
events of 1871 were, in short, the greatest of all knots in the
tangled skein of the revolutionary tradition in France.

France had thereafter to view that tradition through the bitter
experience of these short-lived rebellions, duly suppressed with
much bloodshed by the national executive. The *communards* had
won for themselves something of the glamour of martyrdom
claimed by Babeuf eighty years before: the Commune, too, had
the fascination of the revolution which might have been. But
meanwhile recourse to violence was much discredited. At first
those who still sought reform were offered no clear constitutional
alternative. By them the new Republic of M. Thiers was accepted
at worst with positive resentment, at best with lukewarm caution.
Before long their eyes were to turn to Gambetta, hero of the
national defence, as the rising hope of the stern and unbending
revolutionaries. His influence is the main channel through which
the revolutionary tradition was finally transmitted to the politics
of the Third Republic.

NOTES ON FURTHER READING

A substantial proportion of the literature on the Commune is in the French language and must be omitted here from a list intended for American students. If the student desires a more complete bibliography on the Commune, he may consult Chapter VIII, a bibliographical essay, in my forthcoming *The Revolution of 1870–1871*. Guy Chapman, *The Third Republic of France, The First Phase 1871–1894* (London, 1962) is an excellent survey that contains a useful bibliography.

A very pro-Republican book is John Plamenatz, *The Revolutionary Movement in France 1815–1871* (London, 1952), which has a notably intelligent introduction. As a contrast in viewpoint, see Theodore Zeldin, *Emile Ollivier and the Liberal Empire of Napoleon III* (Oxford, 1963), the last and best word on the subject. One of the major strengths of Michael Howard's *The Franco-Prussian War: the German Invasion of France, 1870–1871* (New York, 1961) is Howard's ability to relate military and political events, making his book a particularly fine transitional study from the Second Empire to the Government of National Defense. Melvin Kranzberg, *The Siege of Paris, 1870–71* (Ithaca, 1950) helps us to understand the temper of the Parisians as disaster overtook them and sets the stage for the Commune.

Frank H. Brabant, *The Beginnings of the Third Republic in France: A History of the National Assembly (February-September 1871)* (London, 1940) remains the best survey of those turbulent months in the Assembly. If somewhat dated, E. S. Mason, *The Paris Commune* (New York, 1930) is important for its use of Russian studies published in Moscow and is an anti-Marxist contemporary of the Jellinek volume noted herein. One of the few studies in English about a revolutionary leader is the reliable Alan B. Spitzer, *The Revolutionary Theories of Louis Auguste Blanqui* (New York, 1957).

To see several aspects of the longterm impact of the Commune, note Jean T. Joughin, *The Paris Commune in French Politics, 1871–1880,* 2 vols. (Baltimore, 1955); and John Roberts, "The Myth of the Commune, 1871," *History Today,* VI, 5 (May, 1957), which presents a brief, intelligent survey based on an excellent understanding of the Commune within the larger framework of French history.